SIMPLIFYING ACCOUNTING LANGUAGE

Jeffrey Slater

Don't lose your balance!

Star

PUBLISHING COMPANY

PUBLISHING COMPANY

940 Emmett Avenue
Belmont, CA 94002

Visit our website at: www.starpublishing.com

Printed in the United States of America

0 9 8 7 6 5 4 3 2 1

ISBN: 0-89863-202-1

Distributed to career colleges by:
H.M. Rowe Companyy
624 N. Gilmor St.
Baltimore, MD 21217

Dedicated to my lovely family: Shelly, Rusty, Abby, Molly, Maggie and Gracie.

CONTENTS

PREFACE

Why was this book written? As a faculty member in an Accounting Department, I constantly heard a consistent criticism from students that accounting textbooks, study guides, or computer tutorials are not really answering all the questions a student may have. My students had great difficulty in simplifying accounting language. I was asked many times to come up with simple definitions, simple examples to back up these definitions, and some type of organization which would get the point across in a clear and understandable manner.

With this inspiration, the birth of *Simplifying Accounting Language* took place. The goal of the book is not to replace an accounting textbook, nor the accounting instructor, nor the accounting supporting material. Once you utilize this book (in class or out) you can then return to your text, to your laboratory assistant or to your instructor and build upon the simplicity that has been presented. Making accounting simple is by no means an easy objective. My format of providing readers with a simplified approach to understanding accounting was developed to benefit:

1. A student in an Accounting I or II course.
2. Those in managerial or advanced accounting courses as a reference to basic accounting theory.
3. A student in Continuing Education and Community Service courses.
4. Students in a Basic Bookkeeping courses.
5. People who have had an Accounting I course but who would now like to review before entering Accounting II.
6. People taking distance learning and Internet courses.
7. Secretaries in offices who would like a quick reference.
8. Businessmen, including salespeople, supervisors and managers as a reference guide.
9. Owners of small businesses.
10. Investors who want a better understanding of stockholder documents that they receive.

The criticisms and needs of students and business people are now being heard and I hope the goal of providing a simple and understandable approach to supplement a basic accounting course will provide you with much satisfaction and reward in your educational advancement—but please, "Don't Lose Your Balance!"

Yes, accounting can be "fun." Feel free to send me your comments or criticism. All letters will be personally answered.

Jeffrey Slater

SPECIAL SUPPLEMENT

**Accounting Review of Accounting I and II:
A Concise Approach**

Area of Coverage in Text	The Situation	Typical Accounts Affected	Category	Rules	Sample Journal Entry That Would Result
Accounting cycle for a service company (transactions)	John Smith invested $10,000 into the Real Estate Agency	Cash J. Smith, Capital	Asset Owner's Equity	Dr. Cr.	Cash 10,000 J. Smith, Capital 10,000
	Paid 2 months rent in advance $500	Prepaid Rent Cash	Asset Asset	Dr. Cr.	Prepaid Rent 500 Cash 500
	Bought office equipment for cash—$300	Office Equipment Cash	Asset Asset	Dr. Cr.	Office Equipment 300 Cash 300
	Bought office supplies on account for $100	Office Supplies Accounts Payable	Asset Liability	Dr. Cr.	Office Supplies 100 Accounts Payable 100
	Sold a home and received a $500 commission cash	Cash Commissions Earned	Asset Revenue	Dr. Cr.	Cash 500 Commissions Earned 500
	Sold a home and will receive a $1,000 commission next month	Accounts Receivable Commissions Earned	Asset Revenue	Dr. Cr.	Accounts Receivable 1,000 Commissions Earned 1,000
	Commissions previously earned were received—$1,000	Cash Accounts Receivable	Asset Asset	Dr. Cr.	Cash 1,000 Accounts Receivable 1,000
	Bought Equipment for $500 paying $60 in cash and charging the balance	Equipment Accounts Payable Cash	Asset Liability Asset	Dr. Cr. Cr.	Equipment 500 Accounts Payable 440 Cash 60
	Agreed to manage a condominium and collected $3,000 in advance	Cash Unearned Management Fees	Asset Liability	Dr. Cr.	Cash 3,000 Unearned Man. Fees 3,000
	Paid balance owed $440 on equipment previously bought on account	Accounts Payable cash	Liability Asset	Dr. Cr.	Accounts Payable 440 Cash 440
	Paid secretary salary $100	Salary Expense Cash	Expense Asset	Dr. Cr.	Salary Expense 100 Cash 100
	John Smith withdrew $50 from the Business	J. Smith, Withdrawal Cash	Drawing (OE) Asset	Dr. Cr.	J. Smith, Withdrawal 50 Cash 50

x

Area of Coverage in Text	The Situation	Typical Accounts Affected	Category	Rules	Sample Journal Entry That Would Result	
Adjusting Entries	Rent expired—$200	Rent Expense Prepaid Rent	Expense Asset	Dr. Cr.	Rent Expense Prepaid Rent	200 	 200
	Supplies Used Up—$150	Supplies Expense Supplies	Expense Asset	Dr. Cr.	Supplies Expense Supplies	150 	 150
	Equipment depreciates $100	Depreciation Exp. Accumulated Depr.	Expense Contra Asset	Dr. Cr.	Depreciation Esp. Equip. Accum. Depr. Equip	100 	 100
	Accured Salaries $50	Salary Expense Salaries Payable	Expense Liability	Dr. Cr.	Salaries Expense Salaries Payable	50 	 50
	Unearned Revenue now earned $1,000	Unearned Revenue Earned Revenue	Liability Revenue	Dr. Cr.	Unearned Revenue Earned Revenue	1,000 	 1,000
Closing Entries	Closed Fees Earned balance into Income Summary (expense and revenue summary) $1,000	Fees Earned Income Summary	Revenue Owner's Equity	Dr. —Cr.	Fees Earned Income Summary	1,000 	 1,000
	Closed hear ($50), telephone ($100) and wages ($500) to Income Summary	Income Summary Heat Expense Telephone Expense Wage Expense	Owner's Equity Expense Expense Expense	—Dr. Cr. Cr. Cr.	Income Summary Heat Expense Telephone Expense Wage Expense	650 	 50 100 500
	Close balance in Income Summary to John Smith Capital	Income Summary J. Smith, Capital	Owner's Equity Owner's Equity	—Dr. Cr.	Income Summary J. Smith, Capital	350 	 350
	Closed $50 in Withdrawal Account	J. Smith, Capital J. Smith, Drawing	Owner's Equity Owner's Equity	Dr. Cr.	J. Smith Capital J. Smith, Drawing	50 	 50
Accounting for a Merchandise Company *	Sold merchandise on credit $5,000	Accounts Receivable Sales	Asset Revenue	Dr. Dr.	Accounts Receivable Sales	5,000 	 5,000
	Customer returned unsatisfactory merchandise $150 (issued credit memo and received a	Sales Returns and Allowances Accounts Receivable	Contra Revenue Asset	Dr. Dr.	Sales Returns and Allowances Accounts Receivable-xxx	150 	
	Sold merchandise of credit $2,000 and sales tax of $100	Accounts Receivable Sales Sales Tax Payable	Asset Revenue Liability	Dr. Cr. Cr.	Accounts Receivable Sales Sales Tax Payable	2,100 	 2,000 100

* See Perpetual inventory System.

Area of Coverage in Text	The Situation	Typical Accounts Affected	Category	Rules	Sample Journal Entry That Would Result	
	Received payment from past sale less discount. ($100 – $2 discount)	Cash Sales Discount Accounts Receivable	Asset Contra Revenue Asset	Dr. Dr. Cr.	Cash Sales Discount Accounts Receivable	98 2 100
	Purchased merchandise on credit $1,000	Purchases Accounts Payable	Cost of Goods Sold Liability	Dr. Cr.	Purchases Accounts Payable	1,000 1,000
	Paid for previous purchase $980 ($1,000 less 2% discount)	Accounts Payable Purchase Discounts Cash	Liability Contra Cost of Goods Sold Asset	Dr. Cr. Cr.	Accounts Payable Purchase Discounts Cash	1,000 20 980
	Returned defective goods $50 (issued a debit memo and received a credit memo	Accounts Payable Purchase Returns and Allowances	Liability Contra Cost of Goods Sold	Dr. Cr.	Accounts Payable Purchase Returns and Allowances	50 50
	Paid Freight Charge on Goods $10	Freight-In Cash	Cost of Goods Asset	Dr. Cr.	Freight-In Cash	10 10
Voucher System	Purchased merchandise $2,000 (gross)	Purchases Vouchers Payable	Cost of Good Sold Liability	Dr. Cr.	Purchases Vouchers payable	2,000 2,000
	Paid for merchandise $1,960 ($2,000 – $40 discount)	Vouchers Payable Purchase Discount Cash	Liability Contra Cost of Goods Sold Asset	Dr. Cr. Cr.	Vouchers payable Purchase Discount Cash	2,000 40 1,960
	Purchased $2,000 of merchandise (recorded at net 2% discount)	Purchases Vouchers Payable	Cost of Good Sold Liability	Dr. Cr.	Purchases Vouchers Payable	1,950 1,950
	Lost discount on purchase recorded at net $40	Discount Lost Vouchers Payable	Owner's Equity Liability	Dr. Cr.	Discount Lost Vouchers Payable	40 4
	Returned defective merchandise $200—received a credit memo	Vouchers Payable Purchase Returns and Allowances	Liability Contra Cost of Goods Sold	Dr. Cr.	Vouchers Payable Purchase Returns and Allowances	200 200
Petty Cash	Established Petty Cash $50 Check #10	Petty Cash Cash	Asset Asset	Dr. Cr.	Petty Cash Cash	50 50

Area of Coverage in Text	The Situation	Typical Accounts Affected	Category	Rules	Sample Journal Entry That Would Result	
	Replenished Petty Cash for $5 bandaids, $15 postage, $10 cleaning Check #15	Bandaids Postage Cleaning Cash	Expense Expense Expense Asset	Dr. Dr. Dr. Cr.	Bandaids Expense Postage Expense Cleaning Expense Cash	5 15 10 30
	During month paid $2 for postage from petty cash	NO ENTRY IS NEEDED AUXILIARY PETTY CASH RECORD COULD BE UPDATED				
	Cash sales today $100 with shortage of $2 (tape more than cash)	Cash Cash Over and Short Sales	Asset Expense Revenue	Dr. Dr. Cr.	Cash Cash Over and Short Sales	98 2 100
	Cash sales $100 with overage of $4 (tape less than cash)	Cash Cash Over and Short Sales	Asset Revenue Revenue	Dr. Cr. Cr.	Cash Cash Over and Short Sales	104 4 100
Bank Reconciliation	Recorded note collection by bank $200 less a collection expense of $5	Cash Collection Expense Notes Receivable	Asset Expense Asset	Dr. Dr. Cr.	Cash Collection Expense Notes Receivable	195 5 200
	Recorded NSF of $1,000 to chargeback John Bill	Accounts Receivable Cash	Asset Asset	Dr. Cr. Cash	Accounts Receivable J. Bill Cash	1,000 1,000
	Record $5 bank service charge	Miscellaneous Expense Cash	Asset Asset	Dr. Cr.	Miscellaneous Expense Cash	5 5
Accounts Receivable (Bad Debts)	Recorded estimated $2,000 in bad debts utilizing the allowance method	Bad Debts Expense Allow for Doubtful Accounts	Expense Contra Asset	Dr. Cr.	Bad Debts Expense Allow Doubtful Acct.	2,000 2,000
	Wrote off uncollectable account of George Marcus $200 utilizing the allowance method	Allowances for doubtful accounts Accounts receivable	Contra Asset Asset	Dr. Cr.	Allow. Doubtful Acct. Accounts Receivable—G. Marcus	200 200
	A/Reinstated account of George Marcus and B/received payment in full of $200	Accounts Receivable Allowance for Doubtful Accounts Cash Accounts Receivable	Asset Contra Asset Asset Asset	Dr. Cr. Dr. Cr.	Accounts Receivable Allow. Doubtful Acct. Allowances Cash Accounts Receivable	200 200 200 200

Area of Coverage in Text	The Situation	Typical Accounts Affected	Category	Rules	Sample Journal Entry That Would Result	
Notes and Interest	Wrote off george Marcus $200 as an uncollectable account	Bad Debt Expenses Accounts Receivable	Expense Asset	Dr. Dr.	Bad Debt Expense Accounts Receivable	200 200
	Bought store equipment with a one year 8% note—$2,000	Store Equipment Notes Payable	Asset Liability	Dr. Cr.	Store Equipment Notes Payable	2,000 2,000
	Gave a 90 day 6% note in settlement of Account Payable $500	Accounts Payable Notes payable	Liability Liability	Dr. Cr.	Accounts Payable Notes payable	500 500
	Bill Flynn paid interest bearing note $550 (principal was $520—interest $30)	Notes payable Interest Expense Cash	Liability Expense Asset	Dr. Dr. Cr.	Notes Payable Interest Expense Cash	1,500 200 2,000
	Moe Black discounteed a $2,000 note at 10%	Cash Interest Expense Notes Payable	Asset Expense Liability	Dr. Dr. Cr.	Cash Interest Expense Notes Payable	195 5 200
	Collected a note $1,000 with interest earned $50	Cash Notes Receivable Interest Earned	Asset Asset Revenue (other inc.)	Dr. Cr. Dr.	Cash Notes Receivable Interest Earned	1,050 1,000 50
	Charges Sheldon Brown's account for his dishonored $600 6% 60 day note	Accounts Receivable Interest Earned Notes Receivable	Asset Revenue (other inc.) Assets	Dr. Cr. Cr.	Accounts Receivable Interest Earned Notes receivable	606 6 600
	Discounted Irene Westing's note ($1,000) at First Bank—Proceeds $990	Cash Interest Expense Notes receivable	Asset Expense Asset	Dr. Dr. Cr.	Cash Interest Expense Notes receivable*	990 10 1,000
	Discounted Sheri Walker's note ($2,000) at Last Bank—proceeds $2,010	Cash Interert Earned Notes receivable	Asset Revenue (other inc.) Asset	Dr. Cr. Cr.	Cash Interest Expense Notes receivable	2,010 10 2,000
	Irene Westing's account is charged for dishonored note plus a protest fee of $5	Accounts Receivable Cash	Asset Asset	Dr. Cr.	Accounts Receivable Cash	1,005 1,005

Area of Coverage in Text	The Situation	Typical Accounts Affected	Category	Rules	Sample Journal Entry That Would Result	
Inventory (perpetual)	Interest accrued on a note $5 by year end	Interest Receivable Interest Earned	Asset Revenue (other)	Dr. Cr.	Interest Receivable 5 Interest Earned	5
	Bought $200 of merchandise on credit	Merchandise Accounts Payable	Cost of Goods Liability	Dr. Cr.	Merchandise 200 Accounts Payable	200
	Sold merchandise on credit for $800 with a cost of $600	Accounts Receivable Cost of Goods Sold Sales Mer. Inventory	Asset Cost of Goods Sold Revenue Asset	Dr. Dr. Cr. Cr.	Accounts Receivable 800 Cost of Goods Sold 600 Sales Merchandise	800 600
Depreciation	Discarded a fully depreciated machine—$2,000	Accum. Dep.—Mach. Machinery	Contra Asset Asset	Dr. Cr.	Accum. Deprec.—Mach. 2,000 Machinery	2,000
	Sold office equipment for $400 having a cost of $750 and acc. dep. of $300	Cash Loss of sales-equipment Accum. Dep. of Equip. Office Equipment	Asset Owner's Equity Contra Asset Asset	Dr. Dr. Cr. Cr.	Cash 400 Loss of sales—Equip. 50 Acc. Dep.—Equip. 300 Office Equipment	750
	Sold office equipment for $600 having a cost of $750 and acc. dep. of $300	Cash Acc. Dep.—Equip. Officer Equipment Gain on sales—equip.	Asset Contra Asset Asset Revenue (other inc.)	Dr. Dr. Cr. Cr.	Cash 1,050 Notes Receivable Interest Earned	1,000 50
	Exchanged old equipment and cash for new equipment— cost of old 1,800 acc. dep. 1,500 cost of new 1,950	Equipment Acc. Dep. Equip. Equipment Cash	Asset Contra Asset Asset Asset	Dr. Dr. Cr. Cr.	Equip. (new) 1,950 Accum. Dep. Equip. 1,500 Equipment (old Cash	1,850 1,650
Payroll	Recorded weekly payroll: Salaries 398.00 Social Sec. 32.00 Medicare 5.77 FIT 32.00 Medical 14.50 Union 11.50 Net Pay 309.55	Salary Expense Social Sec. Medicare FIT Payable Medical Payable Union Dues Payable Salaries Payable	Expense Liability Liability Liability Liability Liability Liability	Dr. Cr. Cr. Cr. Cr. Cr. Cr.	Salary Expense 398 Social Sec. Medicare FIT Payable Medical Payable Union Payable Salaries Payable	24.68 5.77 32.00 14.50 11.50 309.55
	Recorded employee taxes: Social Sec. 24.68 Medicare 5.77 State Unemployemnt 5.50 Federal Unemployment 2.50	Payroll Tax Expense Social Sec. Medicare State Unempl. Tax Federal Unempl. Tax	Expense Liability Liability Liability Liability	Dr. Cr. Cr. Cr. Cr.	Payroll Tax Expense 38.45 Social Sec. Medicare State Unempl. Tax Pay. Federal Un. Tax Payable	24.68 5.77 5.50 2.50

Area of Coverage in Text	The Situation	Typical Accounts Affected	Category	Rules	Sample Journal Entry That Would Result	
	Employer makes monthly deposit Social Security (ee) 29.00 Medicare (ee) 38.00 Social Security (er) 29.00 Medicare (er) 38.00	Social Security Payable Medicare Payable FIT Payable Cash	Liability Liability Liability Asset	Dr. Dr. Cr. Cr.	Social Security Payable Medicare Payable FIT Payable Cash	59 76 32 135
	Employer completes deposit for Federal Unemployemnt Deposit—$125	Federal Un. Tax Cash	Liability Asset	Dr. Cr.	Federal Un. Tax Payable Cash	125 125
Corporations	Sold and issued 200 shares of $100 par value stock	Cash Common Stock	Asset Stockholder's Equity	Dr. Cr.	Cash Common Stock	20,000 20,000
	A/ Received subscription to 5,000 shares at $5 par common stock at $6 per share B/ With down payment of 50% of subscription price	Com. Stock Sub. Rec. Com. Stock Subscribed Prem. Comm. Stock Cash Comm. Stock Sub. Rec.	Asset Stockholder's Equity Stockholder's Equity Asset Asset	Dr. Cr. Cr. Dr. Cr.	Com. St. Sub. Rec. Com. St. Subscribed Premium Com. Stock Cash Com. St. Sub. Rec.	30,000 25,000 5,000 15,000 15,000
	Received balance owed from subscribers and issued 5,000 shares of stock	A/ Cash Com. St. Sub. Rec. B/ Com. St. Sub. Common Stock	Asset Stockholder's Equity Stockholder's Equity Stockholder's Equity	Dr. Dr. Dr. Cr.	Cash Com. St. Sub. Rec. Com. St. Subscribed Common Stock	15,000 15,000 25,000 25,000
	Directors declared a $2 per share dividend on the 10,000 shares of stock outstanding	Retained Earnings Dividend Payable	Stockholder's Equity Liability	Dr. Cr.	Retained Earnings Dividend Payable	20,000 20,000
	Dividend previously declared in now paid	Dividend Payable Cash	Liability Asset	Dr. Cr.	Dividend Payable Cash	20,000 20,000
	Sold 1,000 shares of $10 par common stock at $12 per share	Cash Common Stock Premium Com. Stock	Asset Stockholder's Equity Stockholder's Equity	Dr. Cr. Cr.	Cash Common Stock Premium Com. Stock	12,000 10,000 2,000

Area of Coverage in Text	The Situation	Typical Accounts Affected	Category	Rules	Sample Journal Entry That Would Result	
	Sold 1,000 shares of $10 par common stock at $6 per share	Cash	Asset	Dr.	Cash	8,000
		Dis. on Com. Stock	Stockholder's Equity	Dr.	Dis. on Common St.	2,000
		Common Stock	Stockholder's Equity	Cr.	Common Stock	10.000
	Purchased 200 shares of treasury stock at $120 per share (par is $100)	Treasury Stock	Stockholder's Equity	Dr.	Treasury Stock	24,000
		Cash	Asset	Cr.	Cash	24,000
	Sold and 100 shares of treasury stock at $150 that cost $120 per share	Cash	Asset	Dr.	Cash	15,000
		Treasury Stock	Stockholder's Equity	Cr.	Treasury Stock	12,000
		Contributed Capital	Stockholder's Equity	Cr.	Contributed Capital	3,000
	Sold 100 shares of treasury stock at $100 that cost $120 per share	Cash	Asset	Dr.	Cash	11,000
		Contributed Capital	Stockholder's Equity	Dr.	Contributed Capital	1,000
		Treasury Stock	Stockholder's Equity	Cr.	Treasury Stock	12,000
	Declared a stock dividend (1,000 shares) on $25 par stock. Current market value is $50	Retained Earnings	Stockholder's Equity	Dr.	Retained Earnings	50,000
		Common Stock Distri.	Stockholder's Equity	Cr.	Com. Stock Div. Dist.	25,000
		Premium Com. Stock	Stockholder's Equity	Cr.	Premium on Com. Stock	25,000
	Recorded the distribution of the stock dividend	Common Stock Div.	Stockholder's Equity	Dr.	Comm. Stock Div. Dist.	25,000
		Common Stock	Stockholder's Equity	Cr.	Common Stock	25,000
Bonds	Sold $2,000,000 of bonds at a discount for $1,950,000	Cash	Asset	Dr.	Cash	1,950,000
		Dis. on Bonds Payable	Liability	Cr.	Dis. on Bonds Pay.	50,000
		Bonds Payable	Liability	Cr.	Bonds Payable	2,000,000
	Sold $2,000,000 of bonds at a premium of $2,050,000	Cash	Asset	Dr.	Cash	2,050,000
		Premium Bonds Pay.	Liability	Cr.	Prem. Bonds Pay.	50,000
		Bonds Payable	Liability	Cr.	Bonds payable	2,000,000

Area of Coverage in Text	The Situation	Typical Accounts Affected	Category	Rules	Sample Journal Entry That Would Result
	Paid semi-anual interest on the bonds $15,000	Interest Expense Cash	Expense Asset	← Dr. → Cr.	Interest Expense 15,000 Cash 15,000
	Accrued interest on bonds $5,000	Interest Expense Interest Payable	Expense Liability	← Dr. ← Cr.	Intrest Expense 5,000 Interest Payable 5,000
	Paid interest expense of $3,000 and amortized $250 of the bond premium	Bond Interest Exp. Premium Bonds Pay. Cash	Expense Stockholder's Equity Asset	← Dr. → Dr. → Cr.	Bonds Interest Payable 3,000 Premium Bonds Payable 250 Cash 3,250
	Deposited $5,000 with sinking funds trustee	Bond SInking Fund Cash	Long-term Invest. (asset) Asset	← Dr. → Cr.	Bonds Sinking Fund 5,000 Cash 5,000
	Paid Bonds $100,000 and returned additional cash from sinking fund of $2,000	Cash Bonds payable Bond Sink. Fund	Asset Liability Long-Term Invest.	← Dr. → Dr. → Cr.	Cash 2,000 Bonds Payable 100,000 Bonds Sinking Fund 102,000

DEFINITIONS AND ILLUSTRATIONS

ABSORPTION COSTING

A product-costing method of measuring earnings on the Income Statement in which all manufacturing costs (fixed and variable) are treated as product costs for the units produced.

ACCOUNT

A device or place in an accounting system which records and summarizes the increases or decreases of an individual account, ex: cash, accounts payable, sales, rent expense.

(See: balance column account)

T-Account

Date	Description (accounts)	Folio (PR)*	Debit	Credit	Balance	Dr./Cr.
200X June	4	1	6 0 00		6 0 00	Dr.
	5	1	1 4 0 00		2 0 0 00	Dr.
	10	2		1 5 0 00	5 0 00	Dr.

Account Title   Account #

*PR-Post Reference

$50 is the up to date balance.

ACCOUNTING

A language used to record, summarize, and communicate financial data concerning a person's or company's financial position in an orderly and efficient manner. The computer today is a valuable tool in this process.

Public Accounting	**Private Accounting**	**Government Accounting**
Tax consulting	Internal auditing	OMB
Management consultant	Controller	Department
Auditing	Cost accounting	Individual
	Budgeting	agencies

*(See rules of debits and credits.)

ACCOUNTING CYCLE

During an accounting period the complete *process or procedure used to gather, classify and report useful financial data that* begins *with the recording (journal entries) of transactions in a business and* ends *with the preparation of a post closing (post-clearing) trial balance.*

The Eight Accounting Steps

1. *Journalize transactions* (See journals, journalizing transactions)
2. *Post to the ledger accounts* (See posting)
3. *Prepare a trial balance* (See trial balance)
4. *Prepare a work sheet* (See work sheet)
5. *Prepare financial statements* (See balance sheet, classified balance sheet, income statement, capital statement)
6. *Journalized and post adjusting entries to bring ledger accounts up to date.* (See adjusting entries)
7. *Journalized and post closing entries* (See temporary accounts, closing entries)
8. *Prepare a post-closing trial balance* (See post-closing trial balance)

Note: In a computer system, step 4. is not needed.

4

ACCOUNTING EQUATION*

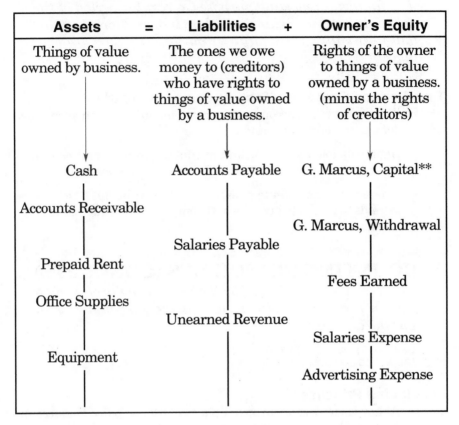

Assets	=	Liabilities	+	Owner's Equity
Things of value owned by business.		The ones we owe money to (creditors) who have rights to things of value owned by a business.		Rights of the owner to things of value owned by a business. (minus the rights of creditors)
Cash		Accounts Payable		G. Marcus, Capital**
Accounts Receivable				G. Marcus, Withdrawal
Prepaid Rent		Salaries Payable		Fees Earned
Office Supplies				Salaries Expense
Equipment		Unearned Revenue		Advertising Expense

*For a corporation see stockholder's equity.
**As revenue capital
As expense capital
As withdrawals capital

ACCOUNTING PERIOD

For financial reporting purposes, a regular period of time which is used to divide and relate information about a business entity during its lifetime

(See fiscal year or calendar year)

Time Periods Could Be: Monthly, Quarterly, Yearly

John went to his accountant to get some information about how long an accounting period is.

John was told by the accountant that the minimum time is usually one month and a possible maximum is one year.

There is no one definite amount of time.* Although 13 four week periods are used to give the best comparisons. A quarter is 13 weeks.

ACCOUNTING PRINCIPLES (CONCEPTS)

Flexible rules established by the accounting profession to help or provide guidelines for a business when it carries out the accounting cycle.

(See principles of… for more detail)
(As well as accounting cycle)

Accounting Principles

Abbey Ellen decided to open up a sweater company. Her accountant told her that a good accounting system should record, process, summarize and communicate information in an orderly and efficient manner (to her stockholders, creditors, ect.)

The accountant gave Abby a book of *accounting principles*, along with the latest newsletters from the accounting board that discussed various *guidelines* or *principles* that Abbey may adopt in carrying out her accounting procedures in preparing her financial reports.

*Most companies operate on a 12 month (or one year) accounting period.

ACCOUNTS PAYABLE

Amounts owed for merchandise or services purchased on credit. (Buy now, pay later!) Accounts payable has a credit balance and is found on the balance sheet.

(See accounts receivable)

Accounts Pay<u>able</u>: Hopefully Able to Pay

Accounts payable has a credit balance and is a liability found on the balance sheet.

ACCOUNTS PAYABLE LEDGER (SUBSIDIARY LEDGER)*

A book or file which contains the records of the individual people *or companies we owe money to. (This book or file is* not *found in the general ledger.)*

If we add up each *individual customer or company account in the subsidiary ledger that we owe money to, the total of all the individual accounts should equal the* one *figure in the controlling account (accounts payable) in the general ledger after postings at the end of the period.*

The sum of the accounts payable ledger (subsidiary ledger) is equal to the one *figure in the controlling account (accounts payable) in the general ledger after postings.*

(See controlling account-accounts payable)

More Bills!! We Owe The Supply Company $5000⁼⁼. Yikes!

*Is arranged in alphabetical order.

ACCOUNTS RECEIVABLE

It is the amount charged or due to a company by its customers from a sale of merchandise or services on account. Accounts receivable has a debit balance and is found on the balance sheet.

(See accounts payable)

Accounts Receiv<u>able</u>: Hopefully We Will Be <u>Able</u> to Receive
Accounts receivable is an asset on the balance sheet.

ACCOUNTS RECEIVABLE LEDGER (SUBSIDIARY LEDGER)*

A book or file which contains the specific or the individual *records of the amount individual* customers owe us. *(This book or file is* not *found in the general ledger.)*

If we add up what each *customer or company in the subsidiary ledger woes us it should equal the* one *figure in accounts receivable in the general ledger (the controlling account)after posting sat the end of the period.*

The sum of the accounts receivable ledger (subsidiary ledger) is equal to the one *figure in the controlling account in the general ledger (accounts receivable) after postings.*

(See controlling account—accounts receivable)

*Is arranged in alphabetical order.

ACCRETION

Increase in economic worth by natural development. Example: Timber orchards grow from seedlings to trees that can be harvested for lumber.

ACCRUAL BASIS OF ACCOUNTING

Net income = revenue earned – expenses incurred (that resulted) in earning that revenue.

Revenues are recognized when services are performed or sales made recurred whether or not cash has been paid out.

(See cash basis of accounting)

Accrual Basis of Accounting
(An example of accrued sales [revenue])

On December 15 1999 Jim Thorpe (owner of Thorpe's Dog Sitting Service) agreed to walk Mrs. Perron's dog for one month. On January 15, 2000, Mrs. Perron will pay Jim $100.

On December 31, 1999 how much revenue has Jim *really earned* from this job? 2 weeks x $25 per week = $50.

So Jim makes an adjusting entry:

Journal   Page #1

Date		Description (accounts)	Folio (pr)	Debit				Credit		
1999 Dec.	31	Accounts receivable-Perron	2	5	0	00				
		Earned revenue	4					5	0	00

Jim's company has earned $50 of revenue although he hasn't received the cash yet.

Remember, *a sale is a sale* under the accrual method when it is earned whether you receive money or not.

(See accrued expenses.)

ACCRUED EXPENSES

Expenses that are accumulating or building up that are not recorded or paid for because payment is not yet due. They really represent an expense in the old year.

(See matching concept)
Reversing entry

```
December, 2004

M   T   W   Th   F
                 26
29  30  31
```

Accrued Expenses

Jim Jackson owns a restaurant. He pays salaries every two weeks as follows:

cook	$400/per week	($80 per day)
receptionist	$100/per week	($20 per day)
waitresses	$200/per week	($40 per day)
Total salaries =	$700/per week	

Of December 26, Jim paid his salaries:

Journal   Page #1

Date		Description (accounts)	Folio (pr)	Debit	Credit
2004 Dec.	26	Salary expense	4	7 0 0 00	
		Cash	1		7 0 0 00

On December 31 2004, Jim wants to adjust or bring up to date the restaurant's true expenses in the old year that resulted in earning those sales in the old year.

He figured he owed salaries as follows for December 29, 30 and 31:

cook	$80 x 3 days	=	$240
receptionist	$20 x 3 days	=	60
waitresses	$40 x 3 days	=	120
			$420

The following adjusting entry was made:

Journal   Page #1

Date		Description (accounts)	Folio (pr)	Debit	Credit
2004 Dec.	31	Salary expense	4	4 2 0 00	
		Salary payable	6		4 2 0 00

Jim will not pay cash for this expense until January (the next payroll), but it is an expense in the year it resulted in earning revenue in the old year.

Key Point: As the expense is incurred a liability results since the obligation has not yet been paid.

ACCRUED INTEREST EXPENSE

Interest (cost of using someone else's money) which is building up *or* accumulating *for which payment is not due, or recorded in our accounting books.*

The interest expense in not *postponed to next year even though we will not pay for it until next year (it is an expense in the old year).*

(See matching concept for further help)

Accrued Interest Expense

Dec. 16, 200X Miro Company needed a loan and went to Glory Bank.

Glory Bank lent $10,000 to Miro at an interest rate of 6% (cost of using the bank's money) for 60 days.

Miro company made the following entry:

Journal   Page #1

Date		Description (accounts)	Folio (PR)	Debit	Credit
200X Dec.	16	Cash	1	1 0 0 0 0 0 00	
		Notes payable	12		1 0 0 0 0 0 00
		(6% 60 days)			

On December 31 200X, Miro wanted to adjust or bring up to date the true interest expense in the old year that resulted in allowing Miro Company to use the $10,000 for 15 days (Dec. 16– Dec. 31)

The following adjusting entry was made:

Journal

Date		Description (accounts)	Folio (PR)	Debit	Credit
200X Dec.	31	Interest expense*	14	2 5 00	
		Interest payable	13		2 5 00

*6% 60 days $10,000 = 1% of $10,000 or $100 (move decimal two places to the left)

6% 15 days $10,000 = 1/4 of $100 or $25

(See 6% 60-day method for further help)

The company *will not pay* the bank the interest until next year, but the 15 days of *interest is an expense in the year it resulted.*

ACCRUED REVENUE

Revenue that has been earned *(that are building up or accumulating) but has not been recorded because money has not been received yet.*

(See accrual basis of accounting)

On December 15, 2000 Rusty Slater (owner of Slater's Dog Walking Service) agreed to walk Mrs. Jones' dog for one monthly. On January 15, 2001 Mrs. Jones will pay Rusty $100.

On December 31, 2000 how much sales (revenue) has Rusty really *earned* from this job?

2 weeks x $25/per week = $50

So Rusty makes an adjusting entry:

Mrs. Jones owes Rusty $50.

Rusty's company has *earned* $50 although he hasn't received the cash yet.

Journal   Page #1

Date		Description (accounts)	Folio (PR)	Debit			Credit		
2000 Dec.	31	Accounts Receivable	3	5	0	00			
		Revenue earned (accru. rev.)	13				5	0	00

Key Point: As accrued revenue is collected accounts receivable will decrease and cash will increase. Revenue is *not* recorded *twice*.

ACCUMULATED DEPRECIATION

A contra asset account on the balance sheet which stores or contains the estimated depreciation expense that is taken when spreading the original cost of a piece of equipment or building over a specific period of time.

As the value of accumulated depreciation increases, it really reduces what the piece of equipment or building is worth on the business's accounting books.

Equipment — accumulated depreciation = worth of equipment on accounting books. The cost amount of this asset indicates the amount that has not yet been depreciated

(See depreciation)

Accumulated Depreciation

Joe Francis bought a new car for $5,000.**

At the time of the transaction, the following value of the car appeared on the accounting books:

Equipment	− Accumulated depreciation	= Worth of equipment on acc. books
$5,000	0	$5,000

*This is called historical cost. It will not change. It represents the actual cost of the equipment.
**(Assuming that the car will depreciate $1,000 for each of the first four years.)

14

After one year the car has depreciated $1,000.

The car is now worth the following on the accounting books at the end of one year:

Equipment − Accumulated depreciation = Worth of equipment on acc. books

$5,000 $1,000 $4,000

After two years the car has depreciated and other $1,000.

The car is now worth the following on the accounting books:

Equipment − Accumulated depreciation = Worth of equipment on acc. books

$5,000 $2,000 $3,000

(The value of the car on the accounting books doesn't always indicate the real value of the car in the real world). A good example is an antique car which has been fully depreciated but is worth more now than when it was first built.

Depreciation is a *paper entry* which *does not effect cash directly,* but does increase a business's expense, rusulting in less profits and therefore, paying less in taxes which is indirectly a cash savings.

Accumulated depreciation

Dr.	Cr.
	1,000 (year 1)
	1,000 (year 2)
	($2,000 balance)

Key Point: Accumulated depreciation, a contra asset is increased by a credit. Accumulated depreciation is found on the balance sheet.

ACID TEST

A financial ratio that measures a company's currrent debt-paying ability. The acid test ratio is: (cash + marketable securities + receivables) ÷ current liabilities.

ADJUSTED TRIAL BALANCE

When the old or original trial balance (list of the ledger) is updated by entries (or what are called adjusting entries) that bring certain accounts in the original trial balance up to date, a new or adjusted trial balance is formed.

(See work sheet)

Adjusted Trial Balance

Before Adjustments Ryan Real Estate Trial balance Dec. 31 200X	Dr.	Cr.	After Adjustments Ryan Real Estate Adjusted trial balance Dec. 31 200X	Dr.	Cr.
Cash	1,000		Cash	1,000	
Prepaid rent	400		Prepaid rent*	300	
Office supplies	300		Office supplies*	100	
Automobile	4,000		Automobile	4,000	
Acc. dep.-auto		1,000	Acc. dep.-auto		2,000
Bill Ryan, capital		6,800	Bill Ryan, capital		6,800
Bill Ryan, drawings	500		Bill Ryan, drawings	500	
Rent expense	100		Rent expense*	200	
Salary expense	1,000		Salary expense	1,000	
Light expense	500		Light expense	500	
			Supplies expense*	200	
			Dep. expense*	1,000	
Totals	7,800	7,800	Totals	8,800	8,800

*been adjusted or brought up to date

16

Three Adjustments

1. During the past year, Ryan Real Estate *used* up $100 of its prepaid rent (or we say $100 of prepaid rent expired).

   If one looks at the trial balance, prepaid rent is too high (it should be $300) or is *overstated* by $100. The following adjusting entry is made to bring the prepaid rent account up to date:

Journal   Page #1

Date		Folio (PR)	Description (acc.)	Debit	Credit
200X					
Dec.	31	10	Rent expense	100	
		5	Prepaid rent		100

2. In checking the office supplies in the real estate office it was calculated that $100 worth of supplies was *left on hand (or $200 of supplies used up).* The following adjusting entry was made: (Adjustments deal with amount used up.)

Journal   Page #1

Date		Folio (PR)	Description (acc.)	Debit	Credit
200X					
Dec.	31	7	Supplies expense	200	
		6	Office supplies		200

3. At the end of the year, depreciation had to be taken on the automobile, ($1,000 per year). When depreciation is taken, it is an *expense* and it also increases *accumulated depreciation.* The following adjusting entry was made:

Journal   Page #1

Date		Folio (PR)	Description (acc.)	Debit	Credit
200X					
Dec.	31	12	Depreciation ex.	1,000	
		4	Acc. dep.-auto		1,000

ADJUSTING ENTRIES

Journal entries at the end of an accounting period when posted which bring up to date certain balances in the ledger accounts at the end of an accounting period to their correct or true balance. These adjustments reflect activities that took place but have not yet been recorded

(See adjusted trial balance)

Adjusting Entries

Ryan Real Estate
Trial balance December 31, 200X

Cash	1,000	
Prepaid rent	400	
Office Supplies	300	
Automobile	4,000	
Accumulated depreciation		1,000
Dill Ryan, capital		6,800
Bill Ryan, Drawings	500	
Rent expense	100	
Salary expense	1,000	
Light expense	500	
Totals	7,800	7,800

Three Adjustments

1. During the past year, Ryan Real Estate *used* up $100 of its prepaid rent (or we say $100 of prepaid rent expired).

   If one looks at the trial balance, prepaid rent is too high (it should be $300) or is *overstated* by $100. The following adjusting entry is made to bring the prepaid rent account up to date:

Journal   Page #1

Date		Folio (PR)	Description (acc.)	Debit	Credit
200X					
Dec.	31	10	Rent expense	100	
		5	Prepaid rent		100

2. In checking the office supplies in the real estate office, it was calculated that $100 worth of supplies was left on hand (or $200 of supplies was used). The following adjusting entry was made:

Journal   Page #1

Date		Folio (PR)	Description (acc.)	Debit	Credit
200X					
Dec.	31	7	Supplies expense	200	
		6	Office supplies		200

3. At the end of the year depreciation had to be taken on the automobile, ($1,000 per year). When depreciation is taken, it is an expense and it also increases accumulated depreciation. The following adjusting entry was made:

Journal   Page #1

Date		Folio (PR)	Description (acc.)	Debit	Credit
200X					
Dec.	31	12	Depr. expense	1,000	
		4	Acc. dep.-auto		1,000

The result is to then make an adjusted or up to date trial balance.

(see adjusted trial balance to see what *new* trial balance looks like)

Key Point: Adjusting entries when journalized and posted allow the financial reports to reflect up to date balances.

ADMINISTRATIVE EXPENSES

Those expenses incurred in the overall management of the company. These expenses are a subdivision of operating expenses.

Example: Rent-adm. building
Dep. exp.—office equipment

AGING ACCOUNTS RECEIVABLE

A list of unpaid customers *accounts which show when their bills are due or how many days their bills are overdue.*

We can use this list to estimate how many accounts will turn into bad debts (not paying their bills)

(See bad debts for more detail; see also schedule of accounts receivable)

Aging Accounts Receivable

List or Schedule of Accounts Receivable by age (when Customers' Bills are Due or Past Due)

Customers Name	Not Yet Due	1-20 Days Past Due	31-60 Days Past Due	61-90 Days Past Due	90 Days Past Due
Smith	$50				
Regan	$60				
Ryan		$25			
Sullivan			$100		
Woodbury				$50	
Keegan					$100
Bernstein					$400

We are concerned that *Sullivan, Woodbury, Keegan, and Bernstein* may never pay their bills. Since the selling terms to these customers were 2/10, N/30 (customers could get a 2% discount if they paid their bills within 10 days of the full amount or the bill was due within 30 days).

It is now later than 30 days for Sullivan, Woodbury, Keegan, and Bernstein. *Our greatest concern is with Keegan and Bernstein.*

ALLOWANCE METHOD FOR BAD DEBTS

A method which estimates the amount of bed debts that will result from charge sales during a period of time (how many people will never pay their bills). The estimates may be based on a % of sales or as a % of accounts receivable.

This method matches bad debt expenses to the period of time when the sales were earned or recognized.

(See direct write-off method)
(See contra account-accumulated depreciation, allowance for doubtful accounts)

Allowance Method for Bad Debts

During last year, Rudy Ricardy Pants, Inc. had charge sales of $10,000, of which $500 or 5% of the charge sales were expected to become bad debts—(customers who did not pay their bills). This %5 figure was based on the past collection records of the company.

Too record this estimated amount of bad debts, the following entry was made at the end of that year:

(Adjusting entry)

Journal   Page #1

Date		Folio (PR)	Description (acc.)	Debit	Credit
200X					
Dec.	31	12	Bad debt expense*	500	
		5	All. for dbtf. ac.		500

(Adjusting entry continues on following page)

Key Point: The allowance for doubtful account has a credit balance and is a reduction in accounts receivable. This allows receivables to be valued as collectible on the balance sheet.

*Also called uncollectable account expense.

(This entry record is the bad debt expense in the same year that sales were earned or recognized.) We don't know which customers will turn out to be bad debts.

In the next year, Paul Lospanato (who had bought some pants *last year*) became a bad debt. The following was recorded to show the bad debt.

	Journal			Page #1	

Date		Folio (PR)	Description (acc.)	Debit	Credit
200X Jan.	15	5	All for dbtf. ac.	XXX	
		3	A/R—Paul Lospanato		XXX

The debit to the allowance account reduces the reserve for bad debts while the credit to accounts receivable reduces what Paul Lospanato owes, since it has bee assumed he will *never* pay it.

(See direct method for comparison)

Key Point: This accounting procedure utilizing the allowance method tries to match credit sales on account to the estimated amounts that contains this estimate of bad debts.

AMORTIZATION

The spreading out (or allocation) the cost of an intangible asset (or bond discount or premium) over the life of the asset (or bonds).

Amortization

Paul Gullette Inc. acquired a patent (an exclusive right) to manufacture and sell a new type of camera.

The cost of the patent was $200,000 (that was recorded as a debit to patents and a credit to cash).

At the end of the first year, the following adjusting entry was made: (Paul Gullette Inc. plans to spread the cost of the patent over a 5 year period at $40,000 per year).

Journal   Page #1

Date		Description (accounts)	Folio (PR)	Debit	Credit
200X Dec.	31	Amortization	10	40,000	
		Patents	5		40,000

This entry will be made at the end of each year until the cost of the patent has been spread (or amortized).

(This same type of entry could be used for goodwill, or organization costs, etc.)

Key Point: As the expense is shown, the asset on the balance sheet decreases.

APPROPRIATION OF RETAINED EARNINGS

A portion or part of retained earnings that is restricted or set aside *for a certain purpose thus making it unavailable for dividend declarations.*

Appropriation of Retained Earnings

Stockholders Equity	
Common Stock, $2 par, 5,000 shares $10,000	
Retained earnings:	
Appropriated retained earnings;	
*For plant expansion $5,000	
For payment of bond debts . 2,000	
For working capital 1,000	
Total appr. retained earnings 8,000	
Unappropriated retained earnings 1,000	
Total retained earnings 9,000	
Total paid-in capital (contributed) and rtd. earnings $19,000	

The journal entry for plant expansion would be:

Journal   Page #1

Date		Description (accounts)	Folio (PR)	Debit	Credit
200X Dec.	10	Retained earnings	14	5,000	
		Retained earnings appropriated for plant expansion	10		5,000

Key Point: Remember retained earnings results from the profit (earnings) that remains in the company.

ARTICLES OF INCORPORATION

The application for the corporations charter.

Includes: Name, location, and purpose of corporation number of authorized shares of stock; classes of shares, voting rights, value of assets paid in by the original subscribers

ASSETS

Things (or properties) of value which make up and are owned by a business. It is the liabilities and capital which show who supplied the assets to the firm. Assets can be expressed and measured in money terms.

(See classified balance sheet)

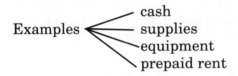

Examples — cash
supplies
equipment
prepaid rent

ASSET TURNOVER

A financial ratio which shows sales divided by total assets.

AUDITING

A procedure to determine if the financial reports of a firm are prepared according to general accounting principles and thus reflect reliable and accurate information

Goals of auditing:
1. Promote efficiency
2. Safeguard assets
3. Reliable information
4. Public confidence
5. System of checks and balances

AVERAGE AGE OF RECEIVABLES

Accounts receivable of a company divided by sales times 365 (accounts receivable ÷ (yearly sales x 365)).

BAD DEBTS

Usually an operation selling expense (or loss) that results when a customer does not pay for some goods or services that were sold on account.

(See allowance method and/or direct method)

Bad Debts

Edward Newburgh, a foreign student visiting America, was able to charge (buy now, pay later) a television set at Flaires Departments Store.

Ed received a letter from his parents asking him to come home immediately.

Ed left America and when he received his bill from Flaires he just *threw it away* (saying he would never return to America).

After many attempts, Flaires decided it wasn't worth the additional cost of trying to *track* Ed down and came to the realization that Ed's bill was a bad debt.

BALANCE COLUMN ACCOUNT

A column in a ledger account which shows a running balance between the debits an the credits. This column summarizes or gives an up-to-date balance *at the time each entry is recorded.*

(See account)

Balance Column Account

Accounts Payable (511)

Date		Item	Folio (PR)*	Debit	Credit	Balance Debit	Balance Credit
200X Jan.	5		PJ 1*		100		100
	15		CP 2**	50			50

*PJ 1—Purchases Journal Page 1
**CP 2—Cash Payments (cash disbursements) Journal Page 2

On January 15, we owe creditors $50.

BALANCE SHEET (POSITION STATEMENT)

A financial Statement which lists or shows the financial position of a business is doing as of a particular date. It gives a history of what is owned *by the business (assets) and what portion of those assets are* owed *by the business (liabilities) and the owner's claim to the assets of the business (owner equity or capital).*

Assets = liabilities + capital (owner equity)*

(See classified balance sheet for a more detailed type balance sheet).

Balance Sheet

The Redstockings**
Balance Sheet
September 9, 200X

Assets		Liabilities	
Cash	$1600.00	Accounts payable	$550.00
Uniform	5000.00		
Automobile	1000.00	Owner's Equity	
Prepaid rent	500.00		
		Ted Villian, capital	1600.00
	———	Total liabilities	———
Total assets	$8210.00	and owner equity	$2150.00

*For a corporation see stockholders' equity.
**Notice the heading answers the questions: who, what, and when.

BALANCING AND RULING

A way in which the accounts in the ledger are cleaned up *or summarized after closing entries have been posted to get ready, as well as, to show that one accounting period is over and a new one is about to begin. All temporary accounts will have no balance brought forward.*

Balance and Ruling

Account: Office Equipment   Account No. 116

Date		Item	PR	Dr		Date		Item	PR	Cr	
200X						199X					
Jul.	18	40	GJ1	100	00	Jul.	31	Adjustment	GJ2	60	00
							31	Balancing	√	40	00
										100	*00*
				100	00					100	00
Aug.	1	Balance Brought Forward	√	40	00						

To start the next accounting period office equipment has a 40 balance

BANK DISCOUNT

The band does not give the borrower the full amount *of the loan because it has deducted the interest (cost of using the bank's money)* ahead of time *instead of waiting until the loan has been paid back and then getting the interest.*

Maturity
Value   –   Proceeds   =   Bank
of   Discount
Note

BANK LOAN

The bank gives the borrower the full amount* *of the loan and collects interest (cost of using the bank's money) when the loan is paid back by the borrower.*

Bank Loan

Art Calnen went to the new Sun Bank to borrow $100,000.

The bank agreed to loan Art the money at an interest of 6%. (Cost of using the bank's money.)

Art left the bank with $100,000

At *maturity* or when the loan came due, Art paid the bank $106,000

$100,000	Loan
+ 6,000	(6% x $100,000)
$106,000	Paid back to bank at maturity

*Keep in mind any loan from a bank is a bank loan even if note has been discounted.

BANK RECONCILIATION

A procedure to explain the difference between the bank balance on the bank statement versus the balance of cash in the ledger (checkbook) of the depositors books

(See outstanding checks)

Bank Reconciliation

This is usually found on the back side of a bank statement.

This bank statement showed a bank balance of $425 but the bank had not processed (or cleared) $300 of deposits we made as well as $140 of checks we've written had not been processed by the bank. So actually the true balance is $585.

On the front side of a bank statement the following information could be found:

1. Last months statement balance
2. Number of deposits made this month
3. Service charges (if any)
4. Ending balance on statement
5. List of all checks and deposits that were cleared (or processed by the bank)
6. Interest earned
7. Account balances for other types of savings accounts
8. ATM Transactions

Checkbook	Bank
–NSF**	
–Service Charges	+to deposit interest***
interest earned	
+-ATMs	–checks outstanding****
+collection of notes	
+-Checkbook errors	+-Bank errors

*Any changes to checkbook will require journal entries to bring cash and other ledger accounts up to date.
**Checks returned due to customers' checking account having insufficient funds to cover the check.
***Deposit not yet processed by bank.
****Checks not yet processed by bank.

30

Lion County
Bank

117 Sadle Road** Lynn, Massachusetts   Telephone—745-1174

This form is provided to help you balance your bank statement

Please notify us of any change in address

Checks outstanding
not charged to account

check number	amount
10	$ 15 00
12	100 00
17	25 00
Total	$140 00

Sort the checks numerically or by date issued.

Check off on the stubs of your checkbook each of the checks paid by the bank and make a list of the numbers and amounts of those still outstanding in the space provide dat the left.

Also verify the deposits in your checkbook with deposits credited on this statement.

Bank balance shown on this statement	$	4	2	5	0	0
Add deposits not credited on this statement		3	0	0	0	0
Subtotal		7	2	5	0	0
Subtract checks outstanding		1	4	0	0	0
Balance: this should be your correct checkbook balance		5	8	5	0	0

If your checkbook does not agree, enter below any necessary adjustment:

Checkbook balance $

Subtract service charge (if any) not entered in checkbook checks paid, but not entered in checkbook

**If no errors are reported to auditor in ten days the account will be considered correct

Subtotal _____

Add $ _____ $ _____

Correct checkbook balance

BEGINNING INVENTORY—MERCHANDISE COMPANY

The amount of goods (merchandise) on hand in a company at the beginning of an accounting period. It is an asset.

The ending inventory at the end of an accounting period becomes the beginning inventory to start the next accounting period.

(See cost of goods sold)

Beginning Inventory—Merchandise Company

This figure for beginning inventory ($19,700) shows the cost to this supermarket for the goods (merchandise on the shelves or in the back room) that it could sell to its customers during the new accounting period before considering additional purchases.

Timothy J. Whelen Supermarket

Income Statement

For year ended December 31 200X

Revenue from sales:		
Sales		$267,736
Less: Sales returns and allowance $2,140		
Sales discount 1,822	3,962	
Net Sales		$263,774
Cost of merchandise sold:*		
Beg. mdse. Inventory, Jan. 1, 200X	$19,700	
Purchases $205,280		
Less purchases discount 1,525		
Net purchases	203,755	
Merchandise able. for sale	$223,455	
Less ending mds. inv. Dec. 31, 200X	22,150	
Cost of merchandise sold		201,305
Gross profit on sales		$62,469

*or cost of goods sold.
**assumed to be sold and thus a cost.
***assumed not to be sold and thus becomes the beginning inventory to start the next accounting period.

BETTERMENT

The process of improving (replacing or repairing assets in a business. Usually at a cost much greater than existing asset. At betterment may make an asset more productive but not necessarily provide a longer life. It is a capital expenditure and not a revenue expenditure.

Key Point: Cost of new motor is debited to machinery.

BOND

An interest-bearing note payable that the borrower issues to lenders. The bond indenture (written agreement) identifies the specifics of the bond provisions.

(See maker for more detail)

Bond

Bernitrone Corporation was deciding whether to issue more stock or sell *bonds* in an attempt to raise more money for plant expansion.

The one thing the management or Bernitrone carefully analyzed was bonds when they reached their maturity date, as well as pay yearly interest on the bonds over the years.

BOND DISCOUNT

The amount that results when selling bonds to investors when the market rate *(effective) is greater than the* bond rate *(contractual). The account bond discount is a debit balance found in the long term liability section of the balance sheet.*

Bond Discount = face value of bond (amount due at maturity before considering interest, payments, etc.) - amount of money investor paid to buy the bonds from a company.

(See bond premium)

Bond Discount

In an attempt to raise money, Marvel Corporation (after going through the proper channels) offered a bond issue of $200,000 at an interest rate (contractual) of 3% annually for 20 years.

This means in 20 years Marvel will pay back:

1. The $200,000 (face amount of the loan) and

2. The interest ($6,000 per year for 20 years or totally $120,000) or the cost of using someone else's money.

When the bonds finally came out to investors, the going market rate for *similar bonds* was a 3 1/2% (effective rate)

Since Marvel bonds paid *less* interest than other bonds of this type, they had to settle for $175,000 (highest bid made by investors). The following entry was made to show the sale of Marvel's bonds:

Journal   Page #1

Date		Description (accounts)	Folio (PR)	Debit	Credit
200X Jan.	5	Cash	1	175,000	
		Discount on bonds	8	25,000	
		Bonds payable	10		200,000

Key Point: Selling price is below the face value.

BOND—FACE VALUE

The amount of a bond that is to be paid at maturity (when it comes due) before considering interest expense, etc., which may have to be paid (or has already been paid).

Bond—Face Value

Brown Inc., issued $1000,000 worth of 6% 20 year bonds to raise money for plant expansion.

Each year Brown Inc. paid $6,000 interest for the use of this money (6% x $100,000 = $6,000 per year).

When the bonds finally came due, Brown Inc. paid back the $100,000 (of the *face value** of the bonds) to the investors.

*The amount stated on the face of the bond.

BOND PREMIUM

The amount that results when selling bonds to investors when the market rate *(effective) is* less *than the bond rate (contractual). The account bond premium is a credit balance found in the long term liability section of the balance sheet.*

Bond Premium = amount of money investors paid to buy bonds from a company - face value (amount due at maturity before considering interest, payments, etc.)

(See bond discount)

In an attempt to raise money Jones Corporation (after going through the proper channels) offered a bond issue of $200,000 at an interest rate (contractual) of 3% annually for 20 years.

This means that in 20 years Jones will pay back:

1. The $200,000 (face amount of loan)

2. The interest ($6,000 per year for 20 years or totally $120,000) or cost of using someone else's money.

When the bonds finally came out to investors the going market rate for similar bonds was 2 1/2% (effective rate).

Since Jones' bonds paid more than other bonds of its type, the company received a did of $225,000 by investors for their bonds (or $25,000 more than they had originally expected). The following entry was recorded to show the sale:

Journal   Page #1

Date		Description (accounts)	Folio (PR)	Debit	Credit
200X Jan.	5	Cash	1	175,000	
		Bonds payable	10		200,000
		Premium on bonds	9		25,000

Key Point: Selling price is higher than face value.

BOOK VALUE—EQUIPMENT

Equipment cost minus accumulated depreciation equals what equipment is worth on accounting books *(book value)*

The equipment may be worth more than book value *in the real world (when it is traded in, sold, etc.).*

(See accumulated depreciation)

Book Value—Equipment

Beth Vernstine, Inc. bought a new truck for $5,000.

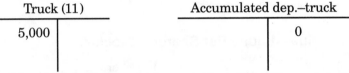

Truck (11)		Accumulated dep.–truck	
5,000			0

At the end of the first year, depreciation of $1,000 was taken on the truck by an adjusting entry:

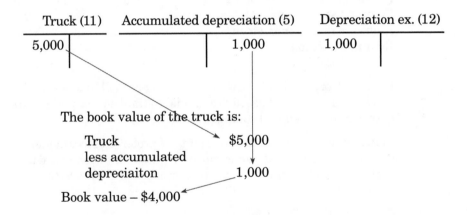

Truck (11)		Accumulated depreciation (5)		Depreciation ex. (12)	
5,000			1,000	1,000	

The book value of the truck is:

Truck $5,000
less accumulated
depreciaiton   1,000
Book value – $4,000

Key Point: Book value represents the net figure in the reporting of assets on the balance sheet.

BOOK VAULE—EQUITY PER SHARE OF STOCK

An estimated value of the claims of a single share of stock in a corporation against the assets of a corporation.

The figure obtained can be very deceptive in that the figure represents an amount that would be given to each stockholders share of stock if a corporation liquidates and doesn't have any expenses, losses, or gains in selling its assets and paying off all the creditors.

(see liquidation/or realization)

Book Value—Equity Per Share of Stock

Fletchers
Stockholders Equity

Preferred 8% stock cumulative, $100 par (100 shard)	$10,000
Premium on preferred stock	2,000
Common stock $5 par (10,000 shares)	50,000
Premium on common stock	5,000
Retained earnings	25,300
Total Equity	$92,300

Fletcher Corporation is liquidating (going out of business) and has a total equity of $92,300 to divide up (find equity per share) between preferred and common stock.

Fletcher, after considering the rights of preferred stockholders (see commutative and participating), states that each share of preferred stock is entitled to $104 per share or totally $10,400 (100 shares x $104 = $10,400).

Common stock is entitled to:

Total equity	$92,300	$81,900	equals $8.02 per
Less Preferred	–10,400	$10,000	share of common
		shares	stock
Remainder to common stock	$81,900 or		

38

BOOKKEEPING

The taking of data and recording them in specially designed form (bookkeeping is only one part of a much larger operation called accounting) as set up by accounting principles.

(See accounting principles)

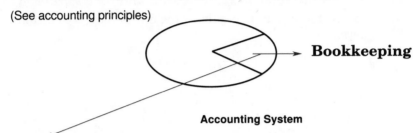

Bookkeeping

Accounting System

One part of the accounting system which helps to record, process, summarize, and communicate information in an orderly and efficient manner.

BREAK EVEN ANALYSIS

That level of business operations for a company where total costs equal total revenue.

BUDGET

A formal financial plan of action for a specified period of time.

BUSINESS ENTITY

A business has an existence that is separate and distinct from its owners, employees, customers, creditors, etc. A corporation is like an artificial person in the eyes of the law.

All entities are units requiring the functions of accounting to be performed.

A Corporation is Like A Person... It Has it's Own Rights Too!

ACME

BY PRODUCT

A joint product that has little sales value in comparison to the products produced in the process. The costs that are assigned to these by products reduce costs of the primary products. Example: wood shavings or metal scraps sold for recycling, or fat from a meat company sold to a soap company.

CALENDAR YEAR

A period of time beginning on January 1 and ending December 31 of the same year. All payroll is based on a calendar year.

(For comparison see fiscal year)

CALLABLE BONDS

A type of bond which allows the company to redeem (or take back) for proper payment *the bond before it reaches its maturity date.*

Callable Bonds

On November 1, 1999 J.P. Slide Company issued $20,000 worth of callable bonds to investors. These bonds would reach maturity (or come due) in 2014.

However, since these are callable bonds, on January 8, 2000, J.P Slide notified the holders of the bonds that the company intended to call back in the bonds (for proper payment) before the maturity date. Why did J.P. Slide do it?

Interest rates were falling and they felt it would be cheaper to recall the old bonds and issue new bonds at a lesser interest rate.

CAPITAL (OWNERS' EQUITY) (NET WORTH)

Rights of the owner to things (assets or properties) owned by a business. If you take assets minus liabilities you come up with the rights of the owner.

(For a corporation, see stockholders' equity)

CAPITAL BUDGETING

A firm's long-range investment in plant and equipment.

CAPITAL EXPENDITURE (BALANCE SHEET EXPENDITURES)

After a business buys a plant asset (building) certain expenditures (costs) will result in order to keep the plant asset (building) at its "full usefulness" as determined by the business.

These expenditures are debited to an asset account (if it is a betterment) or to accumulated depreciation if it is an extraordinary repair. The capital expenditure increases net assets.

(See revenue expenditure)

Extraordinary Repair	$\Longrightarrow$	Betterment
Extends Life	$\Longrightarrow$	Doesn't Extend Life

CAPITAL LEASE

This is a lease that transfers to the lessee most of the risks and rewards that come with property ownership.

Key Point: *Record as an asset and thus can be depreciated over its useful life to the lessee.*

CAPITAL STATEMENT (STATEMENT OF OWNER'S EQUITY)

A statement which shows how the value of the owner's rights to assets in a business have changed from one period of time to another. You take his beginning rights, add to it the companies profile, and subtract his withdrawals: the result being a new figure for his rights or new capital (or owner equity) in the business.

Capital Statement

Sullivan Taxi

Capital Statement

For month ended September 30, 200X

Sullivan capital Sept. 1, 200X		$600,000
Net income fro the month	$50,000	
Less withdrawals	(20,000)	
Increase in capital	_____	30,000
Sullivan capital Sept. 31, 200X		$630,000

Key Point: Remember revenues and expenses go on an income statement and withdrawals are not business expenses and are thus not places on the income statement. Many commercial software packages do not print out the owner's equity section.

CASH BASIS OF ACCOUNTING

(Usually for small company where inventories are not a factor.)

Net income = revenue – expenses

(cash taken in) - (cash going out)

Here we consider:

Revenues are recognized when the cash is received and expense are recognized when the cash is paid out.

Cash Basis of Accounting

Revenue	$160,000*
(Received)	
Expenses	20,000**
Net income	$120,000

*Earned $200,000 on $160,000 collected in cash.
**Expense of $38,000 incurred only $20,000 paid in cash.

CASH DISCOUNT

A savings off the regular price of goods or services due to early payment of a bill by a customer.

If terms of sale were 2/15, n/60 this means:

If you pay your bill within 15 days of the invoice date, (billing date) you can deduct 2% off the bill; in not pay the full amount of the bill within 60 days from the date of the invoice.

(See invoice for clarification)

Cash Discount

John got a bill for $100 in the mail with terms of 2/10, n/60.

He showed the bill to his wife who said, "John, *pay the bill within 10 days* and we can take $2 off our bill; but, if we can't pay the bill within 10 days, make sure you pay the full amount of the bill within 60 days."

To Seller: Cash discount is a sales discount

To buyer: Cash discount is a purchase discount

*2% x $100 = $2.00

CASH DIVIDEND

The amount of cash that a corporation divides or gives out to the stockholders of the corporation, from its earning.

Usually before declaring (or definitely being announced by the corporation that a dividend will be paid) a cash dividend the following is considered:

1. Enough cash
2. Amount of retained earnings which would be used for dividends.

The amount of retained earnings never shows *how much cash the business has available* to pay out in dividends.

(See: Retained earnings, Date of record, Date of declaration, Date of payment for more detail)

Cash Dividend

On May 8, 199X, the board of directors of Howard Slater Inc. *declared* a 50 cent dividend per share on the 50,000 shares of common stock ($10 par) that had been issued. The following entry was made.*

On June 54, the dividend was paid: the entry was recorded as follows:

Journal   Page #1

Date		Description (accounts)	Folio (PR)	Debit	Credit
200X May	8	Retained earnings	10	25,000	
		Cash dividend payable	15		25,000

Journal   Page #1

Date		Description (accounts)	Folio (PR)	Debit	Credit
200X June	5	Cash dividend payable	15	25,000	
		Cash	1		25,000

*50,000 shares x 50 cents = $25,000

CASH DISBURSEMENT JOURNAL

A book or place (journal) which shows the outflow or spending of cash *(check) in recording business transactions.*

(See special journal)

Cash Disbursements Journal
(Cash Payments Journal)
200X
  September

5	Paid Jim Supply Co. what we owed him ($600) less a 20% discount, or $480)
6	Paid Pete's Wholesale Co. $20- we owed them (No discount)
7	Paid $200 for freight to ship some goods

Cash Disbursements Journal

Date	Ck No.	Accounts Debited	Folio (PR)	Sundry Acct. Debited	Accounts Payable Debited	Purchases Discount Credited	Cash Credit
200X							
Sept. 5	2	Jim's Supply Co.	✓		600	120	480
6	3	Pete's Whsl. Co.	✓		200		200
7	4	Freight	215	200			200
30		Total		(200)	800	120	880
				(✓)	(250)	(512)	(110)

(See next page)

Posting Rules   (✓)(250) (512) (110)

Sundry

Total of $200 is not posted!! Place a check (✓)
to show *not* to post total

The freight is posted to the general ledger at
any time during the month as a debit.

When this is done the account number (215)
is put into the post reference column.

Accounts Payable

The total ($800) of the column is posted as a
debit to accounts payable (acc. #250) in the
general ledger at the *end of the month*.

During the month each individual entry (to
Jim's supply and Pete's Whsle.) is posted as a
debit to each account in the A/P subsidiary
ledger.

When this is done, a check (✓) is put in the
post reference column.

Purchase Discount

Total of column $120 is posted as a credit to
purchases discount (acc. #512) in the general
ledger at the *end of the month*.

Cash

Total of column $880 is posted as a credit to
cash (acc. #110) in the general ledger at *end
of month*.

No individual entries are posted during the
month.

CASH RECEIPTS JOURNALS

A book or place (journal) where transactions are recorded when money (check is received from any source. (From a sale, not to a bank, etc.)

Cash Receipts Journal

200X

December	1	Jim Smith paid what he owed us ($100, less a 2% discount, or $98).
	2	Made a sale to Pour Silas for cash of $200.
	4	Borrowed $2,000 cash from a bank.

Cash Receipts Journal

Date	Accounts	Folio (PR)	Sundry Account Credit	Sales Credit	Accounts Receivable Credit	Sales Disct. Debited	Cash Debited
200X							
Dec. 1	Jim Smith	✓			100	2.00	98
2	Paul Silas	✓		200			200
4	Notes Payable	432	2,000				2,000
	Totals		2,000	200	100	2.00	2,298
			(✓)	(25)	(220)	(112)	(110)

Posting Rules
Sundry

Total of $2,000 is not posted!!

Place a check (✓) to show *not* to post total.

Notes payable is posted to general ledger at any time during the month. When this is done, the acc. #432 is put into the folio column.

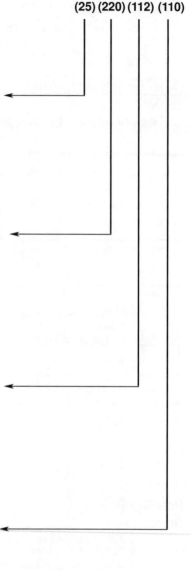

(25) (220) (112) (110)

Sales

Total of column ($200) is posted to sales (acc. #25) as a cr. in the general ledger at the *end of the month*. No individual entries are posted during the month. A check (✓) is put in the folio column to show not to post each amount.

Accounts Receivable

The total of the column ($100) is posted as a credit to a/r in general ledger (acc. #220) at *end of month*.

During the month each individual entry (Jim Smith, etc.) is posted *daily* as a credit to the account, in the a/r subsidiary ledger. When this is done a check (✓) is put in the folio column to show that the posting has been done.

Sales Discount

Total of column ($2.00) is posted as a debit to sales discount in the general ledger (acc. #112) at *the end of the month*. No individual entries are posted during the month.

Cash

Total of column ($2,298) is posted as a debit to cash (acc. #110) in the general ledger at the end of the month. No individual entries are posted during the month.

CASH-FLOW STATEMENT (STATEMENT CASH FLOW)

A statement which shows from what source (or where) the cash has come into the business, as well as where (or for what) cash has been spent by the business.

The result is an increase or decrease in the balance of cash account as of a certain period of time.

(See funds Flow)

Rose Corporation
Statement of Cash Flows
For the Year Ended April 30, 20x2

Cash Flows from Operating Activities

Net Income		$53,700
Add (or deduct) Items Not Affecting Cash Flows		
From Operations		
Decrease in Accounts Receivable	$15,000	
Decrease in Inventory	15,000	
Increase in Prepaid Expenses	(1,800)	
Decrease in Accounts Payable	(3,000)	
Decrease in Income Tax Payable	(1,800)	
Depreciation	57,900	
Interest Expense	8,400	89,700
Net Cash Flows from Operating Activities		$143,400

Cash Flows From Investing Activities

Sale of Furniture		35,100

Cash Flows from Financing Activities

Repayment of Notes payable	$(60,000)	
issue of Common Stock	25,000	
Dividends Paid	(12,900)	
Interest Paid	(8,400)	
Net Cash Flows Used by Financing Activities		(6,300)
Net Increase in Cash Flows		$172,200

Schedule of Noncash Investing and Financing Transactions

Issue of Notes Payable for Furniture	$22,000

CERTIFIED PUBLIC ACCOUNTANT (CPA)

A person who has passed all parts of a state exam qualifying him/her for a license to practice accounting — each state has it's own requirements.

CHART OF ACCOUNTS

A system which shows a classified listing of all the account in the ledger of their respective account numbers being used by an individual business

Chart of Accounts

Account Title	Account Numbers
Assets	
Cash	1
Accounts receivable	2
Land	15
Building	21
Office equipment	29
Liabilities:	
Accounts payable	30
Owner equity:	
Abe Sullivan capital	41
Abe Sullivan, withdrawal	42
Income summary	43
Revenue	
Legal fee	50
Expenses	
Heat	60
Wages	62

Think of a chart of accounts as a table of contents.

CHAIN DISCOUNTS

List price is being reduced by a series of trade discounts.

Example: 10/20/5
Do not combine discounts.

Key Point: These terms are not the result of early payments.

CHECK REGISTER

When a company uses a voucher system the check register (a special journal) takes the place of the cash payments (disbursements) journal.

When a voucher is paid from the check register, the result is to reduce vouchers payable (or what we owe from a bill or obligation) and reduce our cash (write a check).

(See voucher register)

Check Register

Date		Payee (who is receiving money)	Voucher Number	Check Number	Debit Voucher Payable Credit Cash
200X Mar.	10	Katz Realty	3	911	300
	12	Russell Sales	5	912	350
	15	J.P. Stationery	8	913	200

(See voucher register for comparison)

March 10 Paid Katz Realty $300
12 Paid Russell Sales $350
15 Paid J.B. Stationery $200

CLASSIFIED BALANCE SHEET (POSITION STATEMENT)

A balance sheet which subdivides assets and liabilities into specific headings or categories (a more detailed balance sheet).

Assets = current assets + plant and equipment
Liabilities = current liabilities + long-term liabilities

(See: balance sheet for purpose of a balance sheet, long-term investments for another category of assets)

Classified Balance Sheet

Art's Discount Store
Balance Sheet, December 31 200X

Assets

Current assets:

Cash	$1,000	
Notes receivable	500	
Accounts receivable	400	
Merchandise inventory	2,000	
Prepaid insurance	500	
Office supplies	400	
Store Supplies	300	
Total current assets		5,100

Plant and equipment:

Office equipment	$2,000		
Less accumulated depreciation	1,500	$500	
Store equipment	3,000		
Less accumulated depreciation	500	2,500	
Building	2,000		
Less accumulated depreciation	500	1,500	
Land		8,600	13,100
Total plant and equipment			$18,200
Total assets			

Liabilities

Current liabilities: (short-term)

Notes payable	$700	
Accounts payable	2,500	
Wages payable	4,000	
Total current liabilities		$7,200

Long-term liabilities:

First mortgage payable, backed by a mortgage on land and bids		5,000
Total liabilities		$12,200

Owner Equity

Art Irzyk, capital, January 1, 200X		$5,000
Net income for the year ended December 31, 200X	$3,000	
Less withdrawals for personal expenses	(2,000)	
Excess of income over withdrawals		1,000
Art Irzyk, capital, December 31, 200X		6,000
Total liabilities and owner equity		$18,200

CLOSING ENTRIES (CLEARING ENTRIES)

At the end of an accounting period you transfer the balances in all the temporary accounts (revenue, expense, and drawing) and summarize their effects on capital or owner equity. To this one must journalize and then post the closing entries to the ledger.

All temporary accounts will then have a zero balance *when the new accounting period begins.*

Permanent accounts: assets, liabilities, capital (owner equity)

Temporary accounts: revenue, expenses, drawing income summary (expense and revenue summary)

(See income summary)

COMMON-SIZE STATEMENTS

Statements or reports of companies that just show percentages and do not need to use dollar amounts.

(See vertical and horizontal analysis)

Common-Size Statement

Jerves Company Common Size Income Statement For Year Ended December 31, 200X		
	Sales	100%
(Less)	Cost of goods sold	-20%
(Equals)	Gross profit	80%
(Less)	Total operating expenses	30%
(Equals)	Net income	50%

For each dollar of sales 20 cents of it represents a cost of goods sold by Jerves Company. For each dollar of sales 50 cents represent profit or net income realized by Jerves.

These percentages can be used in comparing other companies in the same industry to Jerves.

Closing Entries (Clearing Entries)*

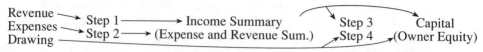

Revenue → Step 1 ———→ Income Summary   Step 3   Capital
Expenses → Step 2 ———→ (Expense and Revenue Sum.)   Step 4   (Owner Equity)
Drawing

Steps	Journal entry to close temporary acct. to I/S (expense and revenue summary)					Accts. that are clsd. (zero blnc.) but will reopen beg. acct. period
Step 1 Sales |1000 →	199X Dec.	31	sales I/S	1,000	 1,000	Sales 1000 | 1000 closed out
Step 2 Rent Expense 500 | Advertising Ex. 200 |	199X Dec.	31	I/S rent ex. adv. ex.	700	 500 200	Rent Expense 500 | 500 Advertising Ex. 200 | 200 closed out
Step 3 Income Summary 700 | 1000 (Step 2) |(Step 1)	199X Dec.	31	I/S capital	300	 300	Income Summary 700 | 1000 300 closed out
Step 4 Drawings** (withdr.) → 200 |	199X Dec.	31	capital drws.	200	 200	Drawings 200 | 200 (Dec. 31) closed out

*If we are doing closing entries for a corporation we would use retained earnings instead of capital.

**Withdrawals are closed since they represent a non-business expense directly to capital.

COMMON STOCK (CAPITAL STOCK)

It is the capital account which summarizes the amount of assets stockholders have invested in the company.

To the investors:

One type of stock (or piece of paper(s) called stock certificates shows the amount of ownership and rights *one has in a corporation.*

The rights usually deal with:

1. Right of one to vote in a corporation
2. Right to share in corporation profit
3. Preemptive right (see definition of preemptive right for more detail)
4. The liquidation process (see liquidation for more detail)

People owning common stock in a company usually have equal rights.

To a corporation:

This is usually a means or way of raising money (capital) by selling shares of stock to investors.

Common Stock (Capital Stock)

Moore Company issued 1,000 share of $10 par common stock to investors at $30 per share.

A. *To an Investor*

One now has bought ownership and rights into Moore Company (depending on amount bought).

B. *To the Corporation*

Moore Company has Raised $30,000 (1,000 shares x $30 per share) by selling common stock.

COMPARATIVE STATEMENTS

Putting reports or statements about a company side by side for two or more periods of time for analysis.

This is done to hopefully interpret or better understand the operation and financial position of a company for a specific period of time (income statement) or as of a certain date (balance sheet).

(See horizontal and vertical for analysis of comparative statements)

Comparative Statements

Joe's Market Comparative Statement For Years Ended Dec. 31, 1999 and 2000		
	1999	**2000**
Sales	$2,000	$1,900
Sales returns and allowances	200	100
Net sales	1,800	1,800
Cost of goods sold	1,400	1,200
Gross profit	400	600
Total operating expenses	300	500
Net income	$100	$100

Although both years show *same profit* compare operating expenses, cost of goods sold, and sales returns and allowances to possibly make some analysis between the two years.

COMPOUND JOURNAL ENTRY

The journal entry in which the transaction is recorded (or placed) into a journal with more than two entries. Debits at the margin, credits indented.

Compound Journal Entry

Date		Account Title	Folio (PR)	Debit	Credit
200X May	1	Cash	1	1,000	
		Supplies	4	50	
		Capital—Gary Wood	10		1,050

CONSOLIDATED FINANCIAL STATEMENTS

Financial statements that show the firm's financial position and income as if they were one single economic entity although they are legally separate companies.

CONSUMER PRICE INDEX

A measure of the general price level of a representative set of consumer items purchased by urdan consumers. A rise in this index is a possible indication of inflation and thus reduced purchasing power of a dollar.

CONTINGENT LIABILITY-NOTES RECEIVABLE

The responsibilities to pay a debt or promise of another person if the first person fails to fulfill his promise or obligation.

(See discounted notes receivable)

Contingent Liability-Notes Receivable

> *"A" Issues Promissory Note Receivable to "B"*
> (1) Jan. 1   "A" promises in writing to bay "B" $100 on June 1.
> *"B" discounts the note receivable*
> (2) Jan. 2   "B" needs money and can't wait until June. "B" goes to the bank to exchange note receivable for cash (not the full amount) with a stipulation* that is "A" doesn't pay off promise on June 1, "B" will pay it to the bank. (*"B" is continentally liable for "A".*)
> *"A" dishonored note receivable*
> (3) June 1   "A" never pays bill to bank
> *Contingent Liability-Notice of Protest*
> ($) June 2   Bank notifies "B" that "B" must pay note receivable that was dishonored by "A".

CONTRA ACCOUNT (ACCUMULATED DEPRECIATION, ALLOWANCE FOR DOUBTFUL ACCOUNTS)

An account (accumulated depreciation, allowance for doubtful accounts, etc.) which is subtracted from its main or associate account (equipment, accounts receivable) in order to show the net or true book value of the main account on the accounting statements of the company.

A. *(Asset)* *(contra asset)* *value of*
   equipment – *accumulated* = *equipment*
   depreciation *on books*

B. *(Asset)* *(contra asset)* *what you expect to*
   accounts – *allowance for* = *collect or realize*
   receivable *doubtful accounts* *from your accounts*

(One should be aware that there are other types of contra accounts besides accumulated depreciation and allowance for doubtful accounts.)

Contra Account (Accumulated Depreciation)
Allowance for Doubtful Accounts

Part of Balance Sheet
A. Current assets"

Cash		$21,600
Accounts receivable	$100,000	
Less allowance for doubtful accounts	2,000	98,000

Part of Balance Sheet
B. Plant and equipment

Store equipment	$10,200	
Less accumulated depreciation	6,000	$4,200
Office equipment	4,000	
Less accumulated depreciation	2,000	2,000

CONTRIBUTION MARGIN
The excess of revenue (sales) over a firm's variable costs. The difference aids in absorbing fixed costs.

Example

Product revenue	$40.00
Variable cost	25.00
Contribution margin	$15.00

CONTROLLING ACCOUNT—(ACCOUNTS PAYABLE)

The account in the general ledger (accounts payable) which, after postings are done, shows the total amount *of dollars we owe people. This one figure is broken down in the subsidiary ledger by showing exactly* who we *owe money to*

The sum of the subsidiary ledger is equal to the one figure in the controlling account (account payable) after postings.

(See accounts payable ledger)

Controlling Account—Accounts Payable General Ledger

Accounts Payable (511)

Date		Item	Folio (PR)	Debit	Credit	Balance Debit	Credit
200X Feb.	29		PJ 1*		900		900
	29		CP 1*	400			500

*PJ = Purchase Journal
*CP = Cash Payment Journal

Accounts Payable Ledger*
(Subsidiary)

Cough Brothers

Date		Item	Folio (PR)	Debit	Credit	Balance Debit	Credit
200X Feb.	10		PJ 1		100		100

Ralph Brothers

Date		Item	Folio (PR)	Debit	Credit	Balance Debit	Credit
200X Feb.	8		PJ 1		200		200
	9		CP 2	100			100

Smith Brothers

Date		Item	Folio (PR)	Debit	Credit	Balance Debit	Credit
200X Feb.	9		PJ 1		600		600
	15		CP 2	300			300

*Not found in general ledger.

CONTROLLING ACCOUNT— (ACCOUNTS RECEIVABLE)

The account in the general ledger (accounts receivable) which, after postings are done, shows the total amount of dollars owed to us. This one figure is broken down in the subsidiary ledger by showing exactly who owes us what.

The sum of the subsidiary ledger is equal to the one figure in the controlling account (account receivable) after postings.

(See accounts receivable ledger)

Controlling Account —Accounts Receivable General Ledger

Accounts Receivable (140)

Date		Item	Folio (PR)	Debit	Credit	Balance Debit	Credit
200X Feb.	29		SJ 1*	1,500		1,500	
	29		CR 1*		1,300	200	

*SJ = Sales Journal
*CR = Cash Receipts Journal

Accounts Receivable Ledger*
(Subsidiary)

Bush and Bee Inc.

Date		Item	Folio (PR)	Debit	Credit	Balance Debit	Credit
200X Feb.	10		SJ 1	500		500	
	18		CR 1		500	———	———

Miller and Company

Date		Item	Folio (PR)	Debit	Credit	Balance Debit	Credit
200X Feb.	4		SJ 1	750		750	
	8		CR 1		550	200	

Mitchell and Mark Inc.

Date		Item	Folio (PR)	Debit	Credit	Balance Debit	Credit
200X Feb.	8		SJ 1	250		250	
	15		CR 1		250	———	———

*Not found in general ledger.

63

CONVERTIBLE BOND

Bonds which may be changed or exchanged for a certain number of shares of stock in the same corporation.

This feature sometimes makes the purchase of these bonds more attractive if the investor thinks the stock price will rise in the future.

Courtesy of E.F. Hutton.

CORPORATION

A company which is considered separate and distinct from its owners (the stockholders) in the eyes of the law. It is incorporated under the laws of the respective state.

(See business entity)

Corporations

Advantage: Limited liability

Easier to raise capital

Going concern.

Note: Capital is now replaced with stock and retained earnings.

COST OF GOODS AVAILABLE FOR SALE
Beginning inventory + net purchases

Found on the classified Income Statement in the cost of goods sold section.

COST OF GOODS SOLD (COST OF SALES)— MERCHANDISE COMPANY
The portion of an income statement which shows the "cost of the merchandise (goods)" a company sold in a specific period of time.

This section is a reduction from revenue (sales) because it shows the cost to the seller *for the merchandise sold.*

We are matching the earned sales of merchandise against the costs and expenses incurred to sell that merchandise.

The difference between revenue and cost of the goods sold is gross profit.

(See accrual basis)

Cost of Goods Sold (Cost of Sales)
A Portion of an Income Statement
Jeep's Apple Market

Sales			XXX
Less Cost of Goods Sold			
1.	Beginning inventory 200X		
2. =	Purchases	$400	$2,000
3. –	Purchase returns	200	
4. =	Net purchases		200
5.	Cost of goods available to sell to customers	$2,200	
6. –	Ending inventory 200X	1,000	
	Cost of goods sold		$1,200

65

Explanation

1. Cost of apples in store (to Jeeps) to start new period of time.
2. Jeeps bought $400 of apples from a farm to *resell* them to customers.
3. Jeeps returned $200 worth of apples, because they were full of worms, to the farm.
4. Actually Jeeps only bought $200 worth of apples after deducting the wormy apples that were returned.
5. Jeeps has $2,200 worth of apples to sell to his customers (this is a cost to Jeeps). You can be sure Jeeps will sell these apples to his customers for a higher price.
6. Out of $2,200 worth of apples $1,000 worth were not sold. This $1,000 of ending inventory will become the beginning inventory for the next period of time.

COST OR MARKET

A traditional accounting practice of pricing ending inventory at what it cost or at the current market price (replacement cost) - whichever one is lower. This practice is based on the accounting principle of conservatism.

Cost or Market

Soap	Cost per Carton to Store	Original Cost to Store	Going Market Rate Now	Cost to Store at Mkt. Rate	Lower of Cost or Market
10 cartons	$5.00	$50.00	$6.00	$60.00	$50.00

Based on this practice the store would price ending inventory at $50 (cost)

COST PRINCIPLE

Record whatever you buy at the price you paid for it *not at the price you* think *its worth. Record at transaction price. The cost principle helps in verifying transaction records if needed.*

COUPON BONDS (BEARER BONDS)

The company issuing coupon bonds usually does not keep *a record of the names and addresses of each bondholder.*

There are interest coupons that are attached onto the bond. Whoever is in the possession of the bond at the time of interest presents a coupon to the company's bank for payment.

Coupon Bonds

Bob Finicharro, owner of a coupon bond transferred ownership of his bond to Paula Corman.

Paula did not have to notify the company because when *interest payments* were due she went to the bank and presented a coupon (which was attached to the bond) *no questions asked.*

(See registered bond for comparison)

CREDIT* (DEBIT, CREDIT)

The right side of any *account or dollar amount which is entered on the right side of the account.*

(See rules of debits and credits)

Credit

Accounts Payable   Account No. 10

Date	Explanation	Folio (PR)	Debit	Date	Explanation	Fol. (PR)	Credit
				200X Sept. 1	Balance		1 0 0 00

(See chart at end of book for specific credit rules)

By rules: A credit will *increase* liabilities, revenue, capital, stock, and retained earnings.

*From Latin derivation credere.

CREDIT BALANCE

The account balance in which the sum of the credits to the account exceeds the sum of the debits to that account.

100	30
200	400
300	430

130 credit balance

CREDIT MEMORANDUM

A form or piece of paper which is used to notify the buyer or seller or merchandise that adjustments are needed on the purchase or sale of merchandise due to pricing mistakes, wrong deliveries, billing errors, damages, etc. The adjustments are mead in the form of a debit or credit memorandum.

For a bank

An addition to the depositors account by a bank.
(See debit memorandum)

General Journal

When a credit memo is issued the result will be to debit sales returns and allowances and credit accounts receivable. (This results on the seller's books.)

On the books of the buyer who receives the credit memo, the result will be to debit accounts payable and credit purchase returns and allowances.

CREDIT CARD EXPENSE

The service charge the credit agency charges for processing credit card sales.

Cash Receipts Journal								
Date	Accounts Credited	PR	Sundry Cr.	Sales Tax Payable Cr.	Accounts Receivable Cr.	Credit Card Expense Dr.	Sales Discount Dr.	Cash Dr.
June 28	American Express (Jeff Jones)				53	2.65*		50.35

Credit Memorandum

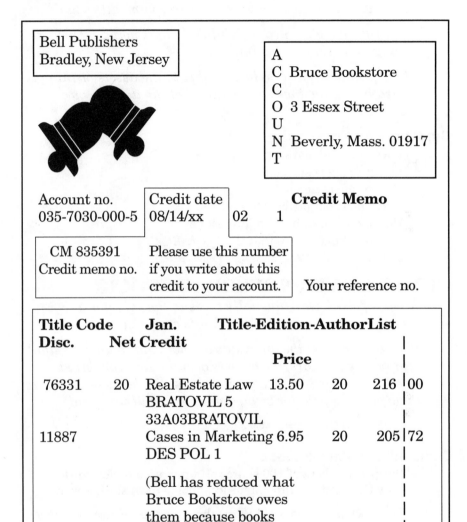

Bell Publishers
Bradley, New Jersey

A
C Bruce Bookstore
C
O 3 Essex Street
U
N Beverly, Mass. 01917
T

Account no.	Credit date		**Credit Memo**
035-7030-000-5	08/14/xx	02	1

CM 835391	Please use this number	
Credit memo no.	if you write about this	
	credit to your account.	Your reference no.

Title Code Disc.	Jan. Net Credit	Title-Edition-AuthorList Price			
76331	20	Real Estate Law BRATOVIL 5 33A03BRATOVIL	13.50	20	216 | 00
11887		Cases in Marketing DES POL 1	6.95	20	205 | 72

(Bell has reduced what
Bruce Bookstore owes
them because books
were returned by
Bruce to Bell)

Page 51008	01	We credit your acct.	421 | 72

CREDITORS

People we owe money to for services or commodities (a debt).

We say we have created a liability by borrowing money or buying an asset on account.

These people (creditors) have rights to the assets or things owned by the business to the extent of the debt we owe them.

Creditors

I needed ten dollars for a date.
I went to my best friend.
He lent me the money.
Today he is not my best friend.
He charged me a buck in interest for
The use of his money, that "Dirty *Creditor.*"

CUMULATIVE PREFERRED STOCK

A type of stock which usually gives to the investor a definite or certain amount of dividends each year.

If for some reason the dividends are not paid (in arrears) that year or in past years, the holders of cumulative preferred stock are entitled to the past or present dividends when future dividends are paid (or before future dividends are paid).

(See noncumulative preferred stock)

Cumulative Preferred Stock

Barry Bluth bought 100 shares of cumulative preferred stock of Biby Corporation through his local home town stockbroker.

The stockbroker had told Barry that this type of stock will pay him a $100 dividend per year.

If the company fails (in arrears) to pay the dividends, Barry will have rights to the past, as well as the present dividends before other types of stockholders (common) in Biby Corporation are paid.

CURRENT ASSETS

Cash or other assets (or things owned by a business) which a company expects to be turned into cash or sold, or used up usually within a year or less through the regular operations of the business.

(See: Classified balance sheet, marketable securities, notes receivable)

Current Assets
A portion of a balance sheet

Assets

Current Assets		
Cash	$500	
Accounts receivable	100	
Supplies	200	
Prepaid insurance	300	
Merchandise inventory	500	
Total current assets		$1,600

CURRENT COST

The cost that would be currently required to obtain the same asset (one previously attained).

CURRENT LIABILITIES

Obligations or services that we owe *that will come due or will be fulfilled usually within a* year *or less. Current assets will be used to pay their liabilities.*

(See notes payable, accounts payable, salaries payable, long-term liabilities)

Current Liabilities

Mike bought a fax machine for his office and charged it (promised to pay later). Thus creating a current liability.

CURRENT RATIO

The total of current assets (cash, supplies, account receivable, etc.) divided by current liabilities (account payable, etc.).

If $\underline{\text{current assets}}$ equaled 2 it would mean that for each
       current liabilities
$2 of current assets there is one dollar of current liabilities in the business. Current ratio measures a firm's ability to pay its debts.

(See classified balance sheet for current assets and current liabilities)

Current Ratio

The current ratio is an indication of the amount of working capital available; this ratio is often compared with the current ratios of similar firms or industry averages. Current ratio includes "less liquid" assets than the "acid test."

Apex Bank had a difficult decision to make as to which company (Jacks or Alls) would receive a short-term loan.*

One reason for the bank giving the loan to Jacks was because

	Jacks	*Alls*
Current Ratio	*3:1*	*1:1*

For each dollar of current liabilities Jocks had three dollars of current assets, while Alls had for each dollar of current liabilities only one dollar of current assets.

It appeared Jack was in a much better position to pay off its debts that Alls (at least in the short-term).

Of course, the current ratio was only *one* factor that the bank analyzed. (In order to come to a decision many factors were investigated.)

*Both in the same type of business.

DATE OF DECLARATION

Day or date that the board of directors of a company announces its intention *to pay a dividend.*

Once this is done the company has created a liability *or it now owes the dividend.*

Date of Declaration

January 8: The board of directors of Doran Corporation declared (announced) a 50 cents cash dividend on its common stock (1,000 shares) payable on February 18 to stockholders of record on January 20. This creates a liability (or what they owe) by Doran Corporation to certain stockholders.

The following entry was made to show the declaration of the dividend:

Journal   Page #1

Date		Description (accounts)	Folio (PR)	Debit	Credit
200X Jan.	8	Retained earnings	3	500	
		Cash dividends payable	8		500

(See date of payment for comparison)

DATE OF PAYMENT

The day or date that a company pays or issues dividends to certain stockholders.

(See date or record for more detail)

Date of Payment

January 8: The board of directors of Doran Corporation declared (announced a 50 cents cash dividend on its common stock (1,000 shares) payable on February 18 to stockholders of record on January 20. When the dividend is paid, the liability (cash dividends payable) will be reduced by paying cash.

The following entry was made on February 18 to show the payment

Journal   Page #2

Date		Description (accounts)	Folio (PR)	Debit	Credit
200X Feb.	18	Cash dividends payable	8	500	
		Cash	1		500

DATE OF RECORD

The day or date that one must be on *the list of stockholders of a company to get or receive a dividend that company has declared.*

(See date of declaration for further help)

Date of Record

January 8: The board of directors of Doran Corporation declared (announced) a 50 cent cash dividend on its common stock (1,000 shares) payable on February 18 to *stockholders of record on January 20.*

The common stockholders, on the company's list (or records), on January 20 will receive a 50 cent dividend per share on February 18 (date of payment).

DAYS IN A MONTH RULE

Thirty days has September, April, June, and November; all the rest have 31 except February, which has 28 and 29 during leap year.

See days in a year table on inside back cover.

DEBENTURE BONDS

The investor buys this type of bond based on the general credit or reliability of the corporation.

Bonds which are sold by a company are not backed up or secured by any asset (*building, equipment, etc.*) *of the company or other companies.*

This becomes important if the company fails to pay off the bond when it comes due.

Debenture Bonds

Jill Hester, holder of a debenture bond, was quite upset when the company failed to honor its obligation.

Jill went to her lawyer who told her that the bond *was not* backed up or secured (since it was a debenture bond) and that he really could not help her. Eventually the corporation went bankrupt and settled on $27 cents on the dollar.

DEBIT (DEBITS, CREDITS)

Left side on any account (or number entered on left side on an account) or dollar amount which is entered on the left side of an account.

(See rules of debits and credits)

| | | | | | | | | Cash | | | | | Account No. 1 | | | | |

Date		Explanation	Folio (PR)		Debit				Date	Explanation	Fol. (PR)		Credit				
200X June	1	Balance		1	0	0	00										

A debit will increase assets, expenses and withdrawals.

(See chart at the end of text for applying debit rule to specific accounts)

DEBIT BALANCE

The account balance in which the sum of the debits to the account exceeds the sum of the credits to that account.

100	30
400	50
500	80

debit balance   840

---

*From the Latin debere; abbreviated dr.

DEBIT MEMORANDUM

A form which is used to notify the buyer or seller of merchandise that adjustments *are needed on the purchase or sale or merchandise due to pricing mistakes, wrong items delivered, billing errors, damaged, etc. The adjustments are made in the form of* debit or credit memorandum.

For a Bank

A deduction to the depositor's account by a bank.

(See credit memorandum)

General Journal
Debit Memorandum

Bell Publishers Bradley, New Jersey

A	
C	Bruce Bookstore
C	
O	3 Essex Street
U	
N	Beverly, Mass. 01917
T	

MD 19491

<u>Memorandum</u> Date Account No. Charge
of debit 11-30-01 35-07030 $338.44

Your account has been charged under this MD number. We will continue to show this charge on your statement until your payment is received or credit is processed.

Your Check No.	Date	Amount of	Your Charge Back#	Dated
4905	11-30-01	$13,519.44	None	------
		Amt. Ded.		
		$338.44		

This charge represents
☒ Returns not credited yet   ☐ Postage
  Bx334464
☐ Price or discount difference ☐ Duplicate deduction of_____
☐ Underpayment   ☐ Your deduction, please send details

(See credit memorandum for journal entry)

DECLINING-BALANCE METHOD OF DEPRECIATION

A method used to spread (or allocate) the total amount of de precaution related to a plant asset (equipment, building, etc.) over its estimated life.

This method takes more, or accelerates depreciation *expense in the early or beginning years (as compared with straight-line) of the estimated life or the plant asset.*

This method does not *consider salvage in the its calculations, except that under this method the plant asset is usually not depreciated beyond whatever the estimated* salvage value is.

(See sum-of-the-years digit method)

Declining-Balance Method of Depreciation

Facts:
1. Cost of truck $5,000
2. 4-year life
3. Rate is 50% (25 is straight-line) or twice straight-line rate
4. At end of the 4th year residual value is approximately $300

Year	Cost	Accum. Depr. at Beginning of Year	Book Value at Beg. of Year (Cost-acc. dep.)	Deprec. (Book Val. at Beg. of Yr. Times R)	Acc. Depr. at End of Year	Book Value At End of Year (cost-acc. dep.)
1	$5,000	0	$5,000 (5,000 – 0) (cost-acc. dep.)	$2,500 (5,000 X 50%)	2,500	$2,500 (cost-acc. dep.) (5,000 – $2,500)
2	$5,000	2,500 (acc. depr. end of yr. 1)	2,500 (5,000 – 2,500) (cost-acc. dep.)	1,250 (2,500 X 50%)	3,750 (2,500 + 1,250)	1,250 (5,000 – $3,750
3	$5,000	3,750	1,250 (5,000 – 3,750)	625 50% X 1,250)	4,375 3,750 + 625	625 5,000 – 4,375
4	$5,000	4,375	625 (5,000 – 4,375)	312.50 (50% X 625)	4,687.50 (4,375 + 312.50)	$312.50

We have not gone below $300.

DEFAULTING—NOTES RECEIVABLE

The process when one who had promised to pay (the maker) a note receivable fails to fulfill his promise at the maturity date. This is called defaulting

(See maker, contingent liability)

Defaulting—Notes Receivable

On June 2 the Bull Bank notified Jim Driscoll that he must pay a note receivable due to the fact Joe Walker diluted (or dishonored his note).

This defaulting meant that Joe didn't pay off his promise when it came due, with the bank turning to Jim Driscoll (who was continentally liable) for payment.

DEFERRAL

Two types:

1. Postponing liability to revenue—*the recognition of revenue (although you have already received the money) until you earn it.*

2. Postponing asset to expense—*the recognition of an expense (although you have already paid for the expense) until you use it up (the asset that is) some or all of the assets are consumed.*

(See accrued expense, accrued revenue)

Deferral

January 1: Spice Magazine received $100 from Pam Sisto for payment of a one year subscription to *Spice.*

Since Spice Magazine hadn't really earned *any* of the sale (until they start sending the magazine) the following entry was recorded by Spice

| | Journal | | | Page #2 | |

Date	Description (accounts)	Folio (PR)	Debit	Credit
200X Jan 1	Cash	1	100	
	Unearned revenue	10		100

Unearned revenue is a liability—Spice *owes* a service to Pam Sisto (a *liability* called unearned revenue). Unearned revenue is a *liability* and not a revenue.

When Spice earns the revenue, or part of the revenue, they will reduce their liability (by a debit to unearned revenue) and will show a revenue (a credit to earned revenue).

Remember unearned revenue is a liability.

Spice Magazine postpones the recognition of a sale until they *earn* it.

DEFICIT—RETAINED EARNINGS

When retained earnings has a debit balance. It is called a deficit.

(See retained earnings)

Deficit—Retained Earnings

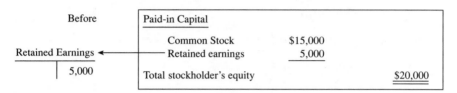

After an $8,000 reduction in retained earnings:

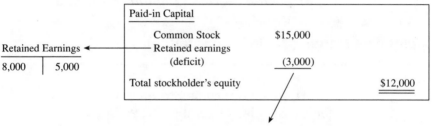

Deficit in retained earnings of $3,000.

DELIVERY EXPENSE

When terms are FOB Destination on the freight, costs for the seller are recorded in the delivery expense account—a selling expense.

Example: If terms were FOB Shipping point freight costs would be part of the cost of goods sold in a Freight-in account.

DEPARTMENTAL MARGIN (CONTRIBUTION MARGIN)

The amount of revenue that an individual *department in a company contributed or adds to the operations of the overall company.*

This amount is calculated as follows:

      Revenue

(Less) *Cost of goods sold*

      Gross Profit

(Less) *Direct expenses (related to that department)*

      Departmental margin (amount of revenue contributed by the department)

Department Margin (Contribution Margin)

Val Company
Portion of an Income Statement
for Year Ended December 31, 200X

	Sweaters	**Sporting Goods**	**Total**
Sales	$20,000	$30,000	$50,000
Cost of goods sold	15,000	20,000	35,000
Gross profit on sales	5,000	10,000	15,000
Direct expenses	3,000	2,000	5,000
Department margin	2,000	8,000	10,000

Out of the $10,000 contributed by the two departments (before indirect expenses—rent, lights, etc.) sporting goods was responsible for $8,000 or $80% of the total company.

DEPLETION

The cost or expense or exhausted resources (mineral, ore, etc.) which are taken from the land during the period.

DEPRECIATION (EXPENSE)

For a particular period of time the amount of asset cost as an expense is called depreciation.

(See accumulated depreciation)

Depreciation

Earl Miller Inc. bought a car for $2,000. At the end of the first year the accountant told Earl to take depreciation on the car for $500.

Cost of car minus accumulated depreciation equals book value of car.

$$\$2,000 - \$500 = \$1,500$$

Insight: Earl told the accountant the car was still as good as new. "So What," said the accountant "depreciation is only a paper entry which will give you more business expenses (when a depreciation is taken it is an expense) and your company a tax break."

DIFFERENTIAL COST

The difference in a firm's cost resulting from a change in levels of production.

DIRECT COSTS

The firm's cost of direct materials, overhead that results in producing a particualr product. Costs that can be traced to a given segment or department.

DIRECT LABOR (MANUFACTURING BUSINESS)

Cost of labor (work) which can be directly related and is specifically charged to certain products that are manufactured (or produced).

I THINK 10 PEOPLE TO MAKE ONE CAKE — IS GOING TO MAKE THIS A PRETTY EXPENSIVE CAKE!

DIRECT MATERIALS (MANUFACTURING BUSINESS)

Cost of material which can be directly related (because it becomes a part of the product) and is specifically charged to certain products that are manufactured (or produced).

DIRECT WRITE-OFF METHOD FOR BAD DEBTS

When a company has decided that a customer will not pay his bill they consider the customer to be a bad debt (an expense) and at this time *shows this expense (or loss) in their accounting books.*

This direct method doesn't try to estimate *what a company's bad debts will be (see allowance method) but this method waits until the bad debt(s) happens.*

Direct Write-Off Method for Bad Debts*

Belle Supermarket usually makes *most* of its sales for cash (therefore the store doesn't try to estimate bad debts).

On January 8 Joe Frank came into the store and asked if he could charge food ($100) due to financial troubles.

The manager, married to Joe's sister, approved the charge.

Three months later, the manager gave up trying to collect the money and called Joe a bad debt expense. The following entry was recorded.

Journal   Page #1

Date		Description (accounts)	Folio (PR)	Debit	Credit
200X					
March	8	Uncollectable account exp.**	10	100	
		Accounts rec.-Joe Frank	5		100

Key Point: This method often overstates revenue in period of time sale is made but understates earnings in the period of time the bad debt is recognized.

*The direct method doesn't use the account entitled allowances for doubtful accounts.
**Some texts use bad debt expense instead of uncollectable account expense.

DISCOUNT ON NOTES PAYABLE

A contra liability account on the balance sheet that reduces notes payable from its face value to the net amount.

Notes payable	5,000
Less: Discount on note	400
	4,600

DISCOUNT ON STOCK

The result of selling stock (or issuing stock) at a price that is less *than par value.*

(See par value for further help)

Discount on Stock

On December 1, 200X the Abby Corporation issued 500 shares of $10 par common stock at $8 per share.

The following entry was made on the company books:

Journal   Page #1

Date		Description (accounts)	Folio (PR)	Debit	Credit
200X Dec.	1	Cash	1	4,000*	
		Discount common stock	18	1,000**	
		Common stock	17		5,000

Key Point: Discount on stock is an account with a debit balance found in the stockholder's equity section of the balance sheet.

(See premium on stock for comparison)

*500 shares x $8 or $4,000.

**Discount on stock was $2 per share or $1,000.

DISCOUNTED NOTES RECEIVABLE

Usually a person or a company who owns a note but needs or wants money now *(can't wait until the maturity date) goes to a bank or finance company to* exchange *the note for cash (which is less than what would have been received at maturity).*

When this happens, it is said that the note has been discounted *by the bank.*

Discounted Notes Receivable

John Wills , on December 1, 200X discounted a $1,000 6% 60 day notes receivable dated November 1, 200X with the bank at a discount rate of 8%

Goal of problem

How much money will John get from the bank?

Steps	Explanation

Step 1-Find maturity value
1. Face value of the note = $1,000
   + interest on note = 10
   maturity value = $1,010
	Maturity value= what the bank will receive when the person or company (maker) pays off the note on December 30. (Nov. 1-Dec. 30 = 60 days)

Step 2-Find discount Dec. 1. to Dec. 30 = 30 days	Discount time = the number of days the bank will have to wait until the note comes due (after taking the note from John). This number of days helps the bank figure what it should charge John for discounting the note.
Step 3-Find discount on Maturity value $6.73 (8% x 30/360 x $1,010)	Discount = amount bank charges for waiting 30 days for the note to come due. This discount is based on a rate time number of days before note is paid times maturity value.
Step 4-Find proceeds $1,003.27 $1,010. - $6.73 = ⟨ $1,003.27 ⟩ (Maturity—Discount) (value on note)	What John gets when he discounts the note. John settled for $1,003.27 instead of $1,010 if he could have waited until Dec. 30 and not discounted the note.

DISCOUNTS LOST

The net price method records the purchases after deducting the cash discount before payment. If a discount is missed an account called discounts lost results.

Discounts lost-reported as non operating expense at bottom of the income statement. This account shows when a cash discount was missed.

DISHONORED NOTES RECEIVABLE

Failure or refusal of a person (maker) to pay a note (or what he owes when it is due (maturity date).

Dishonored Notes Receivable

On March 1, John Scrivano promised, in writing, to pay the order of Ken Phillips $100 on June 1 of that same year.

On June 1, the note had now been *dishonored* by Scrivano, who had no intention to pay back Ken Phillips.

DIVIDEND

A distribution of assets in the form of cash, or company stock, or property, etc., that a corporation divides or gives out to the stockholders of the corporation (each type of stock may receive different amounts of dividends from its profits.)

This amount is determined by the corporations board of directors. A dividend does not have to be paid each year.

(See cash dividends and stock dividends for more detail)

DIVIDEND IN ARREARS

Dividends which are owed to cumulative preferred stock-holders that have not *been paid* by the company.

(See cumulative preferred stock for further help)

Dividend in Arrears

Neal Goldman bought 100 shares of *cumulative preferred stock* of APC Corporation through his local home town stockbroker.

The stockbroker had told Neal that this type of stock will pay him a $100 dividend per year.

If the company fails or is late (in arrears) in paying the dividend, Neal *will have rights to the past as well as present* dividends before other types of stock (common stock) are paid.

DOUBLE-ENTRY BOOKKEEPING

The requirement in accounting that requires that each transaction *be recorded* in at least two accounts *(the result being the total of the debits is equal to the total of the credits).*

(See bookkeeping, rules of debits and credits, accounting equation)

Double-Entry Bookkeeping

Jan. 8 Bopel Motors bought a car from GMV Corporation for $3,000 (for resale to its customers).

The following entry was recorded in Bopel's journal:

Journal   Page #1

Date		Description (accounts)	Folio (PR)	Debit	Credit
200X Jan.	8	Purchases	500	3,000	
		Cash	1		3,000

The general ledger (when posted) shows:

General Ledger

Cash (1)

Date		Item	Folio (PR)	Debits	Credits	Balance Debits	Credits
200X Jan.	1		1	5,000		5,000	
	8		1		3,000	2,000	

Purchases (500)

Date		Item	Folio (PR)	Debits	Credits	Balance Debits	Credits
200X Jan.	8			3,000		3,000	

EARNINGS PER SHARE

A calculation which shows how much profit or earnings the corporation is making per share (or for each share) or stock.

$$\frac{\text{Total profit (net income) after taxes}}{\textit{Total number of shares of stock (outstanding)}}$$

Earnings Per Share

"Special News Release"

It was reported by Duane Dell, president of Toyland Inc., that 200X was record year for sales and earnings.

Mr. Dell reported sales reached $500,000 with net income hitting an all time high of $200,000 after taxes.

Duane went on the say that since the company had only 1200,000 shares of stock outstanding, the companies showed *earnings per share of $2 ($200,000 NI).*

$$\frac{}{\text{100,000 shares}}$$

EMPLOYEE

A person who is hired (employed) by a company or person for wages or salary.

Employee

Jeff Frank works for Mingle Motors as a mechanic. Jeff is an *employee* of Mingle Motors.

(See employer)

EMPLOYER

A person or company who hires (employs) others to work in a company for wages or salary.

Employer

Stop and Hop, a corporation, is the *employer* of many thousands of workers (stock clerks, managers, meatmen, etc.).
(See employee)

EMPLOYEE'S EARNING RECORD

A form which contains all the payroll information that has been accumulating or building up *about an employee or worker in a business for the* calendar year *(January 1 to December 31)*

(See: employers payroll taxes, net pay [for employee taxes])

		Hours Worked		Total	Deductions					Net Pay	Check No.	Cumulative Pay
	Week #	Regular	Overtime	Earnings	Soc. Sec.	Medicare	Fed. Inc.Tax	State Inc.Tax	Med. Ins.			
												5362500
	40			137500	8525	1994	22200	6875	4400	93506	710	5500000
	41			137500	8525	1994	22200	6875	4400	93506	750	5637500
	42			137500	8525	1994	22200	6875	4400	93506	780	5775000
	43			137500	8525	1994	22200	6875	4400	93506	812	5912500
	44			137500	8525	1994	22200	6875	4400	93506	830	6050000
	45			137500	8525	1994	22200	6875	4400	93506	842	6187500
	46			137500	8525	1994	22200	6875	4400	93506	871	6325000
	47			137500	8525	1994	22200	6875	4400	93506	893	6462500
	48			137500	4805	1994	22200	6875	4400	97226	915	6600000
Total 4th Quarter				1787500	73005	25922	288600	89375	57200	1253398		
Total for Year				7150000	405480	103688	1154400	357500	228800	4900132		

The earnings record is broken into 4 13-week quarters.

EMPLOYER'S PAYROLL TAXES

The employer pays:

1. *FICA (Federal Insurance Contributions Act)*—The employer matches the total amount of FICA contributed by its employees. Congress sets the rate and salary base used in the calculations of FICA.
2. *Federal Unemployment Compensation*—the employer pays the tax. The employee does not. This tax is to help people who have become unemployed.
3. *State Unemployment Compensation Tax*—the employer pays the tax in most states. If the employer has provided stable employment to his workers the business in some states receives a reduced rate.

(See Federal Deposit coupon employee's earning record, payroll register)

		GENERAL JOURNAL				
Nov	30	FICA — Social Security Payable	203	4 3 1 89		
		FICA — Medicare Payable	204	1 4 2 77		
		Federal Income Tax Payable	205	7 8 4 00		
		Cash	111		1 3 5 8 66	
		To record the Form 941 tax deposit for week				
		#47 payroll on November 25, 19XX				

Employer's payroll tax expense equals the sum of (1) Social Security (2) Medicare (3) Federal Unemployment and (4) State Unemployment.

Social Security Payable
Medicare Payable
FUTA
SUTA

> All liabilities on the balance sheet with credit balances

Payroll Tax Expense—Expense with a debit balance on the income statement

ENDING INVENTORY—MERCHANDISE COMPANY

The amount of goods (merchandise) on hand in a company at the end of an accounting period.

(See beginning inventory, cost of goods sold. For calculating ending inventory, see LIFO, FIFO, weighted average, gross profit method, or retail method)

Ending Inventory—Merchandise Company

This figure of ending inventory ($22,150) shows the cost to Jim's Supermarket for the goods (merchandise on the shelf or in the back room) that was *not* sold to its customer during an accounting period.

This cost of ending merchandise is subtracted from the cost of the goods available for sale.

This ending inventory becomes the beginning inventory in the next accounting period (then it will become a part of the cost of the goods sold by Jim's Supermarket).

Jim's Supermarket
Income Statement
for Year Ended December 31, 200X

Revenue from sales
Sales $267,736
Less: . . . . Sales returns and allowances $2,140
Sales discount 1,822 3,962
Net Sales $263,774
Cost of merchandise sold:
Merchandise inv. Jan 1, 199X $19,700
Purchases $205,280
Less purchases discount 1,525
Net purchases 203,755
Merchandise available for sale 223,455

Less ending merchandise inv. Dec. 31, 200X**	22,150

Cost of merchandise sold. 201,305
Gross profit on sales $62,469

*Assumed sold and thus a cost.
**Assumed not sold and thus becomes beginning inventory.

EQUITIES

The rights or claims of others to things (assets or properties) owned by a business including both the rights of the owner (called capital of owner equity) and the rights of the customers we owe money to (called creditors or liabilities). The creditors and owner have supplied the assets to the business.

(See accounting equation, balance sheet, stockholders equity)

Equity

Assets = Equities

Liabilities + Capital (owner equity)

EQUIVALENT UNITS

Used in process costing to calculate how the dollars of costs are allocated between the finished goods and the goods in process. Example: a unit 60% complete has only 60% of the labor cost charged to it as compared to a finished good of 100%.

EXPENSES

Costs of assets consumed in operating or running a business to produce revenues.

(See matching concept)

An expense may be recognized even though not paid. Example: heat house in August, don't pay bill until September— still an expense in August. Expenses are temporary accounts recorded on the income statement. They have a debit balance.

EXPIRED COSTS

Costs which have been used up *(or assets consumed) in running or operating a business.*

(See prepaid for further help)

Expired Costs

Mike bought a life insurance policy good for five years (for $200.00). At the end of the first year $40.00 or one-fifth of the insurance, had *expired or been used up.*

Mike now only has four years of life insurance.

EXTRAORDINARY ITEMS

Unusual *happenings or transactions in a business that greatly affect the financial condition of the business.*

These unusual transactions are not the typical activities that normally happen in running the operations of the business.

(See transactions for details)

FACTORY OVERHEAD—MANUFACTURING BUSINESS

Costs in a manufacturing business that do not relate directly into the making of the finished product.

Factory overhead equals the total of all manufacturing costs in a company minus the sum of direct material and direct labor include rent, heat, insurance, etc.

Note: Raw materials and direct labor are not included in factory overhead.

FICA* (SOCIAL SECURITY AND MEDICARE) FEDERAL INSURANCE CONTRIBUTION ACT

A deduction from a persons gross pay which is used for federal programs involving the aged, health insurance, disabilities, etc.

The employer is required to match the Social Security and Medicare contribution of the employee.

There is a maximum that can be deducted each year based on a percentage of the earnings (as determined by Congress), for Social Security. There is no base cut off for Medicare. The "base cut off" (wage base limit) is subject to annual changes.

(See employer's payroll taxes, gross pay, net pay, payroll register)

Assume: Social Security Rate 6.2% on $76,200
Medicare 1.45% No Base

Employee	Earnings	Wage Base Limit	Rate	$
Social Security	150,000	76,200	.062	4,724.40
Medicare	150,000	none	.0145	2,175.00

FEDERAL TAX DEPOSIT COUPON

Coupon that is completed when an owner of a company makes periodic deposits to pay FICA, Social Security and Medicare of employees and employer along with any FIT due of the employee. Back of form 941 lists specific deposit requirement.

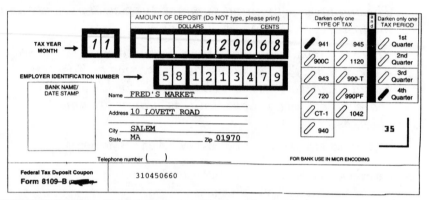

FINISHED GOODS INVENTORY ACCOUNT—MANUFACTURING COMPANY

One type* of inventory account in a manufacturing business that contains cases of goods or merchandise that are ready to be sold.

The costs of direct materials, direct labor, and factor overhead make up the cost of finished goods.

(See direct labor and factory overhead)

Key Point: Finished goods inventory is a current asset on the balance sheet.
*The other two types of inventory: 1. raw materials: 2. work in process (goods in process).

100

FIRST-IN, FIRST-OUT (FIFO)

A method used to assign or place a cost or dollar figure on the ending inventory in a business.

This method assumes the ending inventory is made up of the latest or most recently purchased items.

It is assumed that the first goods brought into a store will be the first goods sold.

The flow assumes that the old merchandise in a store is sold before the new . So if anything is left in the store at the end of a period of time, we assume it is newer merchandise.

(See LIFO, and weighted average)

First-In, First-Out
J.J. Supermarket

Old		No. of Cans of Soup Bought for Resale (to Customers)	Cost Per Can	Total Cost
On	January 1, 200X	20	$3.00	$60.00
	March 1	15	2.00	30.00
	November 3	10	1.00	10.00
	November 10	<u>55</u>	<u>2.00</u>	<u>110.00</u>
New		100		$210.00

If at the end of the year 10 cans of soup are left in the store, the cost of these cans are calculated as follows:

$2.00 × 10 cans = $20.00

Cost of ending inventory

→ Cost of goods sold = $190

(See weighted average and last-in, first-out for comparison)

FISCAL YEAR (ACCOUNTING YEAR)

A one year accounting period. The year can start at any time but must meet the requirement of 12 consecutive months. Many companies use January 1 to December 31. But, to repeat, it is not mandatory to start the year on January 1. A fiscal year could fall on the same time as a natural business year. For example, a car dealer's business year is October 1 to September 30.

(See calendar year for comparison)

FIXED ASSETS (PLANT ASSETS, TANGIBLE ASSETS, NONCURRENT ASSETS)

Things of value owned by a business (usually not *for resale) that have a* long life *can be used in the production or sale of other assets or services. Assets which will produce revenue for more than one fiscal period.*

Examples include: building, land and equipment.

(See classified balance sheet)

FIXED COST

Any cost whose total remains constant as the activity of the operations of the company changes

FIXED LIABILITIES

Obligations that we owe that will not be due for a year or more. When they become due within a year, they become current liabilities.

(See classified balance sheet)

Fixed Liabilities

Ed Noon wanted to buy a house. He went to the bank to borrow $15,000.

Ed received the loan with the condition stating his loan would *not come due* for five years.

A *fixed liability* was created.

FOB DESTINATION (FREE ON BOARD)

The seller of the goods is responsible to pay *the transportation costs (freight) involved with getting the good(s) to the buyer (or reaching the buyer's destination).* Usually seller retains ownership until goods are received by the purchaser.

(For comparison, see FOB shipping point, delivery expense)

FOB SHIPPING POINT (FREE ON BOARD)

The buyer *of the goods* is responsible to pay *the* transportation costs *(freight) involved with getting the good(s) from the seller (or his shipping point).* Usually buyer assumes ownership as soon as goods are shipped.

(For comparison, see FOB destination)

FREIGHT-IN

As account in the periodic system which shows the trans- portation costs *(or shipping charge) the purchaser (buyer) is responsible for.*

Freight-in represents a part of the cost of the goods (merchandise) bought or purchased. Some people add the cost of the freight right on to the purchase account. This applies to purchase of merchandise only.

Freight-In

Fred Finger, manager of Toys Inc., bought $500,000 of purchases (or toys for resale to his customers) from a toy wholesaler.

In order to get the toys (purchases) Fred had to pay a shipping (transportation) charge of $1,000 since terms were FOB shipping point.

Fred made the following entry:

Journal   Page #1

Date			Description (accounts)	Folio (PR)	Debit	Credit
200X Jan.	5		Purchases	10	500,000	
			Freight-in	5	1,000	
			Cash	1		501,000

(Both debits represent a *cost* to Toys Inc. Both accounts will show up on Toy's income statement.)

(See cost of goods sold)

Key Point: Freight-in account is a debit balance which will be found on the income statement.

FUNDS

Funds = current assets – current liabilities.

Funds are also called net working capital. Sources of funds increase net working capital. Uses of funds decrease net working capital. Funds could also relate to cash such as petty cash funds.

(See fund statement)

Funds

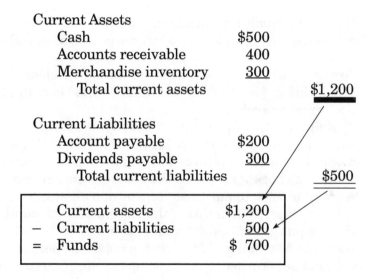

Current Assets
Cash	$500
Accounts receivable	400
Merchandise inventory	300
Total current assets	$1,200

Current Liabilities
Account payable	$200
Dividends payable	300
Total current liabilities	$500

	Current assets	$1,200
−	Current liabilities	500
=	Funds	$ 700

GENERAL JOURNAL

Usually a book or place (journal) where miscellaneous transactions are recorded that do not fit into special journals (sales, purchases, cash receipts, cash disbursements, and check registers). A general journal will help link together debit and credit parts of transactions.

(See: sale, purchase, cash receipts, cash disbursement and check register)

General Journal

Date		Description (accounts)	Folio (PR)	Debit	Credit
200X Sept.	4	Accounts Payable-Ralph Bros.	✓ 511	200	
		Purchases returns & allow.	212		200
	9	Sales, returns & allowances	210	500	
		A/R Mitchell and Mark	✓ 200		500

Sep. 4 Received a credit memorandum from the Ralph Brothers for defective merchandise, $200 (three postings needed).

Post:

    1. To accounts payable (as a debit) in the general ledger. When this is done the account number (511) is put in the post reference column.

    2. To Ralph Brothers in our accounts payable subsidiary ledger to show we don't owe Ralph Brothers as much money (because we returned some purchases). When this is done, a check(✓) is put in the post reference column.

    3. A credit of $200 to purchase returns and allowances in the general ledger. When this is shown, the account number (212) is put in the post reference column.

Sep. 9 Issued to Mitchell and Mark Inc. a credit memorandum for merchandise returned. Credit memo No. 45, $500 (three postings needed).

Post:

    1. A debit of $500 to sales returns and allowances in the general ledger. When this is done, the account number (210) is put in the post reference column.

    2. To accounts receivable subsidiary ledger to show they don't owe us as much money (because they returned some goods or services to us). When this is posted, a check (✓) is placed in the post reference column.

GENERAL LEDGER (PRINCIPAL LEDGER)

The book or place that contains the income statement and balance sheet accounts. (It is in order of the chart of accounts.)

A list of the general ledger accounts and balances forms a trial balance.

(*See subsidiary ledger for comparison—accounts payable or accounts receivable)

General Ledger (Principal Ledger)**

Cash (1)

Date		Item	Folio (PR)	Debits	Credits	Balance	
						Debits	Credits

Store Supplies (2)

Date		Item	Folio (PR)	Debits	Credits	Balance	
						Debits	Credits

Purchases (500)

Date		Item	Folio (PR)	Debits	Credits	Balance	
						Debits	Credits

*Subsidiary ledgers are not in the general ledger.
**The general ledger is numbered based on account numbers and is not paged as a typical book would be.

GOING CONCERN CONCEPT

As assumption in accounting that a business entity will function (or not go out of business) for an indefinite or indeterminable number of years.*

(See business entry)

*This is one reason why creditors are willing to supply assets to a business and accept payment at a future date.

GOODWILL

An intangible value which results in an excess amount paid for a company over the value of net assets.

This results when expected future earnings (or earning power) of the company is in excess of the normal or usual rates of return of other companies in that industry.

(See intangible assets)

> *Why?*
> Good customer relationships
> Location
> Employee morale
> Product superiority
> Managerial skill
> Business reputation
> Remember goodwill in an intangible asset.

GROSS PAY

The amount of money earned by a worker in wages before all deductions (taxes, social security, etc.) are taken out.

Gross pay is what we wish we could take home.

(See net pay for comparison)

What They Pay Me is Gross Enough, But After Taxes...

GROSS PROFIT (GROSS MARGIN)

The amount of money earned* *(which is collected or will be collected) from the sale of goods minus the cost of the "goods" we have sold.*

Gross Profit (Gross Margin)

Jeep's Apple Market
(A Portion of an Income Statement)

Revenue

1.	Gross sales		$5,000
2.	Less: sales returns	$1,000	
3.	Net sales	4,000	

Cost of Goods Sold

4.	Beginning inventory 200X	$2,000	
5.	+ Purchases $400		
6.	– Purchase returns 200		
7.	Net purchases	200	
8.	Cost of goods available to sell	$2,200	
9.	Ending inventory	1,000	
	Cost of goods sold		1,200
10.	Gross profit		$2,800

Remember, a sale is a sale, under the accrual method of accounting, when it is earned, whether money is received or not!

Explanation

1. Total dollars spent by customers in buying apples from Jeep's (charge as well as cash) $5,000
2. Customer returned $1,000 worth of apples due to worms that were found in those apples.
3. Total sales minus the returns by the customers ($4,000).
4. Cost of apples in store (to Jeeps) to start new period of time ($2,000)
5. Jeeps bought $400 of apple from a farm to *resale* to customers.
6. Jeep returned $200 worth of apples because they were full of worms.
7. Actually Jeep only bought $200 worth of apples after deducting wormy apples.
8. Jeep has $2,200 worth of apples to sell to his customers (this is a cost to Jeeps who sells them at a higher price).
9. Out of $2,200 worth of apples $1,00 were not sold. This will become the beginning inventory for the next period.
10. Before such expenses as heat, wages, etc., Jeeps apple market showed a gross profit of $2,800.

Don't forget, it will be gross profit less operating expenses that will equal net income.

GROSS PROFIT METHOD

A method used by a business to estimate a cost or dollar figure for ending inventory.

This method assumes the business knows its average (usual) gross profit percentage $\frac{gross\ profit}{net\ sales}$

which is used in trying to estimate a figure for ending inventory.

(For comparison see: LIFO, FIFO, weight average, and retail method of costing ending inventory)

Gross Profit Method

Given:	Net sales =	$5,000
	Gross profit =	30% of net sales
	Net purchases =	$4,000
	January 1 beginning inventory =	$10,000

What is the goal? Get an estimated cost of ending inventory on Jan. 31.

Steps

1. Remember: net sales − cost of goods sold = gross profit
   $1,500 (30% x $5,000)
2. Cost of goods sold equals $3,500 (net sales) $5,000 - gross profit ($1,500)
3. Cost of goods sold equals

Beginning inventory	$10,000
+ Net purchases	4,000
Cost of goods available to sell	$14,0000
− Ending inventory	?
= Cost of goods sold	$3,500

4. To reach our goal what number must be subtracted from $14,000 (cost of goods available to sell) in order to get $3,500?

$$\$14,000 \ - \ \boxed{10,500} \ = \ \$3,500$$

Estimated cost of ending inventory January 31.

GROSS SALES

The total revenue (cash and / or charge sales) made by a business in running its operations for a specific period of time.

(See accrual and cash basis accounting, gross profit)

Gross Sales

Jim's Supermarket Income Statement for Year Ended December 31, 200X		
Revenue from sales (Gross sales)		$70,000*
Less: Sales discounts	$5,000	
Sales Returns & Allowances	3,000	8,000
Net sales		$62,000

Gross sales is what Jim wished he had but net sales is what he must be satisfied with.

Key Point:

gross sales

— sales discount

— SRA

= Net Sales

*This could be all cash or partially cash and accounts receivable

HORIZONTAL ANALYSIS OF STATEMENTS

One way of understanding or interpreting comparative statements.

This method shows the rate and amount change across columns of statements from period to period.

This way will hopefully give a better understanding of the operations and financial position of a company as of a certain date.

(See comparative statements for more detail)

Horizontal Analysis (Across Columns) of Statements

Joe's Market
Comparative Statement
for Years Ended December 31 1998 and 1999

	1999	1998	Am't of Change	Rate*
Sales	$2,000	$1,900	+100	+ 5.26%
Sales returns and allowances	200	100	+100	+ 100%
Net sales	$1,800	$1,800	0	
Cost of goods sold	1,400	1,200	+200	+ 16.63%
Gross profit	$400	$600	−200	− 33.3%
Total operating expense	300	500	−200	− 40%
Net income	$100	$100	0	

*Change base 1997

$$5.26\% = \frac{+100}{1,900}$$

116

INCOME STATEMENT (EARNINGS STATEMENT, OPERATION STATEMENT)

Earned revenue (sales) - incurred expenses = profit or loss.

We match the amount of money earned (which is collected and / or will be collected) from the sale of goods or from service performed, against the expenses incurred (or that resulted) in earning that revenue for a specific period or time.

If sales are greater than expenses a profit is made.

If expenses are greater than sales a loss results.

(See matching concept)

Income Statement

John's Cleaners
Income Statement for Year Ended December 31, 200X

Revenue $20,000

Operating expenses:
    Cleaning wages $8,000
    Water and electricity 500
    Rent expense 800
    Cleaning supplies expense 500
    Depreciation expense-cleaning equipment . 1,000

    Total operating expenses 10,800

Net income $9,200

For an income statement for merchandise company see gross profit on p. 112.

INCOME SUMMARY (EXPENSE AND REVENUE SUMMARY) ACCOUNT

The temporary account* to which all revenues, costs and expenses *are closed or transferred to at the end of the accounting period.*

The balance of income summary account is then closed or transferred to the capital account.

All revenues and expenses, *as well as income summary, will then have zero balances to start the next accounting period.*

*Permanent accounts would be assets, liabilities, capital, retained earnings etc.
(See closing entries)

Income Summary (Expense and revenue summary)

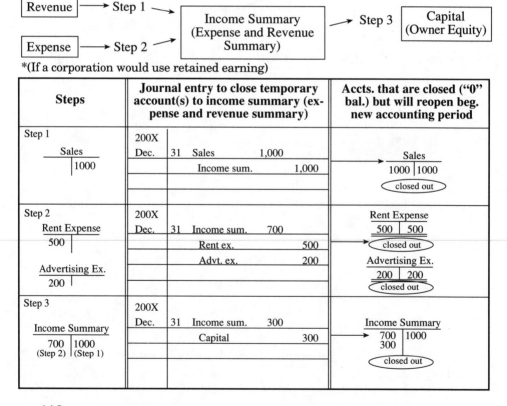

*(If a corporation would use retained earning)

Steps	Journal entry to close temporary account(s) to income summary (expense and revenue summary)	Accts. that are closed ("0" bal.) but will reopen beg. new accounting period

Step 1
 	
Sales
    | 1000
	200X
	Dec. 31 Sales 1,000
	           Income sum. 1,000
		Sales
		1000 | 1000
		(closed out)

Step 2
 	
Rent Expense
500 |
 	
Advertising Ex.
200 |
	200X
	Dec. 31 Income sum. 700
	          Rent ex. 500
	          Advt. ex. 200
		Rent Expense
		500 | 500
		(closed out)
		Advertising Ex.
		200 | 200
		(closed out)

Step 3 Income Summary 700 | 1000 (Step 2) | (Step 1)	200X Dec. 31 Income sum. 300 Capital 300	Income Summary 700 | 1000 300 (closed out)

INDIRECT COST

Cost which is not easily identified as a certain department's and thus is spread among departments.

INFLATION

A general increase in the average prices of goods and services over time.

ARE YOU SURE THIS HOUSE IS WORTH $500,000! WHEN I THOUGHT ABOUT BUYING IT 3 YEARS AGO IT WAS ONLY $214,000. YIKES!

INTANGIBLE ASSETS

Noncurrent assets which have a long life which have no physical appearance which will produce revenue for more than one fiscal period due to exclusive privileges and rights.

(See goodwill)
Intangible Assets

Goodwill

Trademarks

Copyrights

Patents

Franchises

INTEREST

Cost of using someone else's money.

(See discounting notes receivable)
Interest

Paul needed some money for doing his Christmas shopping.

He went to BC loan company and borrowed $100 for 1 year at a 10% interest rate.

When the loan came due (maturity date), Paul paid BC $110.

($1000 + [10% x $100 or $10])

($10 of which was the interest (or the cost of using someone else's money.)

INTERIM STATEMENTS

Statements that are prepared or made in between or during *the fiscal year (a 12-month period of time).*

This is done for management, which wants to know how the company is doing during the year without having to wait 12 months to get the year-end results.

Interim reports may be prepared monthly, or every three months, etc. It depends on the demand of the people wanting the information.

Interim Statement
Neptune Company
Income Statement
for month Ended June 30, 200X

Sales	$1,000
Less cost of goods sold	500
Gross profit	$500
Less operating expensed	200
Net income for month	$300

(Since this company makes 12 interim income statements, the final yearend statement will summarize the *12 individual* statements)

INTERNAL CONTROL

A method or system used by a business to control such things are fraud, stolen goods, inaccurate figures, etc., in its operations.

The internal control system (if efficient) allows management to get a "true picture" of its business position at a given point of time.

Small expensive items may be on display at a cash register, but instead of being on stock shelves the items are picked up at a special pick-up counter. This also is done at some home improvement centers where very large items are picked up at a drive-up area.

(See vouchers, check register)

INVENTORY TURNOVER

The financial statement ratio that shows cost of goods sold divided by average inventory.

INVOICE

A statement or bill showing a list of all goods and services bought or sold.

(See purchase order)

Invoice

TERLIN CORRUGATED BOX CO., INC.				INVOICE			
15 RALPH ROAD							
SALEM, MA 01970				NO	5638		
TELEPHONE: 745-1174				DATE	11/9/9X		
				YOUR ORDER NO.			
SOLD TO ● RUSSELL SEAFOOD INC.				SHIPPED TO			
● 21 ATLANTIC AVENUE							
● SALEM, MA 01970							

OUR ORDER #1132	SALESMAN	TERMS 1% - 10, NET - 30		FOB DEST.	DATE SHIPPED	SHIPPED VIA	
QUANT. ORDER.	QUANTITY SHIPPED	STOCK NO. / DESCRIPTION	UNIT PRICE		UNIT	AMOUNT	
	1,400	12-8 OZ. SHRIMP	84	85	M	118	70
	700	12-16 LB. ONION RINGS	158	10	M	110	67
			TOTAL			229	37

Seller—Sales Invoice

Buyer—Purchases Invoice

JOB COST CARD

Basically the work in process account's subsidiary ledger. Costs of a particular job are accumulated on this job cost card / sheet.

JOB ORDER COST-ACCOUNTING

Manufacturing costs are assigned to each job(s) in a perpetual inventory system.

JOURNAL

Book or place where transactions are first *put or recorded.* The process of putting transactions into a journal is called journalizing.

The transactions are placed into the journal in chronological order (January 1, 2, 8, 10 etc.)

The journal links the debit and credit portions of a transaction together.

(See special journals)

I'm Sure When I Bought Supplies, I ordered Heating Equipment...

CAPTAIN LOG

JOURNAL ENTRY

The transaction that is recorded into a journal. Debits at the margin: credits indented. An explanation of the transaction may be included.

Journal Entry

Journal   Page #1

Date		Account Titles	Folio (PR)	Debit	Credit
200X Sept.	1	Office Equipment		500	
		Cash			500
		(bought epuipment for cash)			

JOURNALIZING TRANSACTIONS

The process of placing or recording transactions in a journal (a book or place where transactions are first put, or recorded from) source documents such as bills, sales slips.

Journalizing Transactions*

Transaction:
Bought truck for business with cash ($1,000).

General Journal

Date		Account Titles	Folio (PR)	Debit	Credit
200X Sept.	1	Truck		1,000	
		Cash			1,000

Don't forget to ask yourself...
1. What accounts are affected?
2. What are their categories?
3. Are the accounts increasing or decreases?
4. What are the rules of debit and credit?

*For a special journal sample see cash receipts journal.

LAND IMPROVEMENTS

Attachment to land that has limited life and is subject to depreciation.

Example: Driveways, parking lots, fences, sprinkler systems, gates etc.

LAST-IN, FIRST-OUT (LIFO)

A method used to assign or place a cost or dollar figure on the ending inventory in a business.

This method tries to match revenue and expenses by assuming the newest merchandise in a store is sold before the older merchandise *in the store so if anything is left, we assume it is the* older *merchandise.*

The last goods brought into the store are the first goods to be sold.

This method assumes the ending inventory is made up of the earliest *purchases made by the business.*

(See matching concept)

Last-In, First-Out
J.J. Supermarket

		No. of Cans of Soup Bought for Resale (to Customers)	Cost Per Can	Total Cost
Oldest on (Earliest)	January 1, 200X	20	$3.00	$60.00
	March 1	15	2.00	30.00
	November 3	10	1.00	10.00
Newest (Latest)	November 10	<u>55</u>	<u>2.00</u>	<u>110.00</u>
		100		$210.00

If at the end of the year 10 cans of soup are left in the store, the cost of these cans are calculated as follows:

$3.00 x 10 cans=$30 cost of ending inventory

cost of goods sold = 180

(See weighted average and first-in, first-out comparisons)

Key Point: When prices are rising LIFO results in lower income and thus a tax savings.

LEASE

Contract to rent property the lessee obtains the right to posses and use the property from the lessor.

1. Capital lease

2. Operating lease

Key point: Any physical alteration to the leased property in which benefits will extend beyond the current accounting period are called LEASEHOLD IMPROVEMENTS that can be amortized over the period of time.

LEDGER (GENERAL)

All the accounts of a company grouped together. Usually transactions are first recorded into a journal and eventually posted (or information transferred) to a group of accounts called ledger.

The ledger is arranged by account numbers and is based upon the chard of accounts. In the ledger book each account is a new page.

(See accounting cycles)

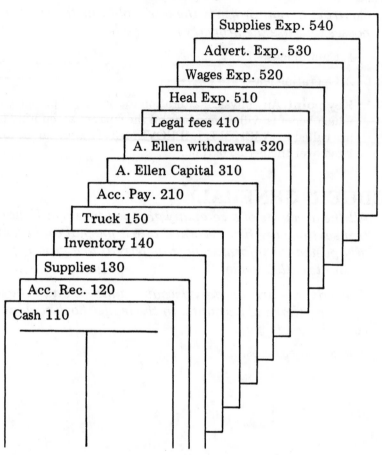

General Ledger

Supplies Exp. 540
Advert. Exp. 530
Wages Exp. 520
Heal Exp. 510
Legal fees 410
A. Ellen withdrawal 320
A. Ellen Capital 310
Acc. Pay. 210
Truck 150
Inventory 140
Supplies 130
Acc. Rec. 120
Cash 110

LIABILITIES (CREDITORS)

Debts or obligations owed by a company from borrowing money for services.

(See: accounts payable, promissory note, on account, current liabilities, long-term liabilities)

		Normal Balance
Example:	Accounts Payable	Cr.
	Notes Payable	Cr.

LIMITED LIABILITY

The corporation is responsible for its debts and obligations.

(For comparison see unlimited liability)

Limited Liability

Jim's Sporting Goods (a corporation) opened for business on Jan. 1, 1991.

On June 1, 2001 Jim's Sporting Goods faced heavy losses and was forced to declare bankruptcy.

Jim, who owned a beautiful home and car, didn't have to worry about the creditors going after him for the *company's* losses.

LIQUID ASSETS (QUICK ASSETS)

Assets that can be turned into cash quickly.

(See marketable securities)

Liquid Assets (Quick Assets)

Cash

Notes Receivable

Accounts Receivable

Marketable Securities

Interest Receivable

Rent Receivable

LIQUIDATION—PARTNERSHIP

The winding-up process of a company that is going out of business.

The winding-up process includes:

1. Selling the assets of the company
2. Paying the creditors (liabilities)
3. Giving whatever cash or assets are left to the owners of the business (this results after first paying the creditors)

(See realization-partnership)

Liquidation-Partnership

Carolyn Bergstrom Hair Stylists

Cash	$10,000	
All noncash assets	60,000	
All liabilities		$10,000
T. Duffy capital		20,000
C. Bergstrom capital		20,000
C. Peterson capital		20,000
Total	$70,000	$70,000

Sold all noncash assets for $90,000 showing a gain on realization of $30,000 ($90,000 - $60,000 = $30,000). ⟶

The following entries show the sale of the noncash assets and the rest of the liquidation process:

1.	Sale of Assets:		
		Debit	Credit
	Cash	90,000	
	Assets		60,000
	Gain on realization . . .		30,000

1.	Division of Gain to Capital:		
		Debit	Credit
	Gain on realization	30,000	
	T. Duffy, capital		10,000
	C. Bergstrom, capital . .		10,000
	C. Peterson, capital . . .		10,000

2.	Payment of Liabilities:		
		Debit	Credit
	Liabilities	10,000	
	Cash		10,000

3.	Distribution of Cash to Capital:		
	T. Duffy, capital		30,000
	C. Bergstrom, capital . . .	30,000	
	C. Peterson, capital	30,000	
	Cash		90,000

After Realization		
Cash	$100,000	
All liabilities		$10,000
T. Duffy capital		30,000
C. Bergstrom capital		30,000
C. Peterson capital		30,000

(Noncash assets are off the books)

131

LONG-TERM INVESTMENTS (ASSETS)

Assets which are accumulated by a firm to be held on a long term basis. These assets are not directly used in producing the revenues of the firm.

(For comparison see marketable securities)

Long-Term Investments (Assets)

A Portion of a Balance Sheet
Moll Corporation
Balance Sheet
Dec. 31, 200X

Current Assets:

Cash $1,000
Accounts Receivable 2,000
Inventories 4,000
(At Lower of Cost (FIFO) or Market)

Total Current Assets $7,000

Long-Term Investments:

Investment in Mayberry Co. . . . $3,000

Total Long-Term Investments $3,000

Plant Assets:

LONG-TERM LIABILITIES

Obligations or services that we owe that will not be due for a year or more. When they become due within a year, they become current liabilities. Example: bonds payable.

(For comparison see current liabilities)

Long-Term Liabilities

A Section of a Balance Sheet

Assets

_____
_____
_____
_____
_____

Liabilities

Current Liabilities:

Notes Payable	$5,000	
Accounts Payable	2,600	
Wages Payable	400	
Total Current Liabilities		$8,000

Long-Term Liabilities

Mortgage Payable	5,000	
Total Liabilities		$13,000

Capital (Owner Equity)

LOOK-BACK PERIOD

An IRS rule; the IRS looks at the amount of taxes paid on Form 941 during the period beginning on July 1 and ending on June 30 and determines if an employer is to be a monthly depositor or a semi-monthly depositor. The payroll tax deposit rules and deadlines are different for monthly and semi-monthly depositors.

The determination is based upon the dollar amount of Form 941 taxes paid in the past year. To pick the deposit status for 2000 the IRS would "look-back" at the period between July 1, 1998 and June 30, 1999. The employer's status is evaluated every year.

LOWER-OF-COST-OR-MARKET

Inventory values are priced at the lower of its historical cost or its current replacement (market value).

LCM can be applied to each inventory item or to the total inventory. It is assumed that as the purchase price falls so will the selling price fall.

MAKER

A person or company who (in writing) definitely promises to pay to the order of someone (payee) a definite sum of money at a fixed future date.

The person or company making the promise is the maker.

(For comparison see payee)

Maker

$3,000		Dayton, Ohio October 2 19 9X
90 Days	After Date	I Promise to Pay to
The Order of	Mets Electronic Co.	
Three-Thousand	---	Dollars
Payable at	McQuire Bank	
Value Received with Interest at	6%	
No. 20 Due December 1, 199X	*William E. Ford, Jr.*	
	(Maker)	

MANUFACTURING COMPANIES

Companies that produce products from materials they buy for sale to final customers or other companies.

Example: Sneaker manufacturer (Nike)

Shoe manufacturer (Bass)

MARGINAL COST

The additional cost associated with producing one more unit of a product.

MARKETABLE SECURITIES

Temporary investments made by a corporation that has some idle or extra cash on hand to buy income yielding securities (stock, bonds, etc.) which can be quickly turned back into cash when needed.

When the corporation needs the money to carry on the normal operations of the business it will sell the securities.

(See long-term investments for comparison)

Marketable Securities

A Portion of a Balance Sheet
Vac's Corporation
Balance Sheet
Dec. 31 200X

Current assets:

Cash		$5,000
Marketable securities, at cost	500	
(market price $600)		
Merchandise inventory	1,000	
Prepaid rent	400	
Total current assets		$6,900

MATCHING PRINCIPLE (REVENUE AND EXPENSES)

An accounting principle that takes all the revenue (sales) earned* in a specific accounting period and subtract all expenses which have arisen, or been incurred in earning that revenue.

The result will be to match revenue earned as compared to expenses and costs involved in earning that revenue—the net result being profit or loss.

(See operating statement)

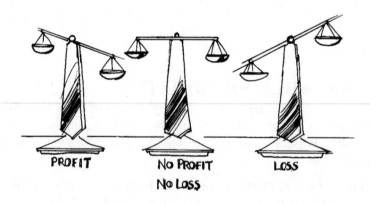

PROFIT   No PROFIT   LOSS
                No LOSS

*The scales relate to height and not weight.

MATURITY DATE

The time or date when a note (a written promise to pay) becomes due.

Maturity Date

Jan. 1   Bob Singer needed a loan to buy a car.

Jan. 2   Bob borrowed $1,000 from BC Loan Company promising in writing to pay back the $1,000 plus $100 in interest on December 31 to BC Loan Company.

Dec. 31   *Maturity Date*
Bob paid BC Loan Company $1,100 ($1,000 + $100)

$1,000 = principal
$100 = interest

*under an accrual system in accounting, a sale is recognized and recorded when it is earned whether you receive the money or not.

MERCHANDISE COMPANY

A business that sells to customers goods or merchandise that are ready for sale in order to earn revenue or sales.

Net Sales

– Cost of goods sold

= Gross profit

– Operating expenses

= Net income

(See cost of goods sold—merchandise company)

MERCHANDISE INVENTORY — (MERCHANDISING COMPANY)

Goods on hand in a merchandise business which are for resale to its customers.

This merchandise, or goods available to sell, is usually sold within one year to those customers.

(See LIFO, FIFO, weighted average, cost of goods sold)

We Started This Year With Great Enthusiasm & A Great Inventory! Well—We Still Have The Inventory.

STOCK ROOM

MINIMUM LEGAL CAPITAL (LEGAL VALUE)

Usually it is the par or stated value of the stock that is issued by a corporation that must be kept in the business for protection of the creditors.

Each state has its own regulations for legal capital.

(See par value)

Minimum Legal Capital

Fox Corporation issued 3,000 shares of common stock ($1.00 par) to investors.

The state in which Fox operated requires that the company keep $R3,000 as legal capital ($1.00 x 3,000 shares) in the business for possible protection of the creditors (since the stockholder is only liable to the amount of his investment in the company).

Key Point: When dividends are issued they cannot reduce permanent contributed capital below minimum legal capital as required by state law.

MORTGAGE NOTES PAYABLE

The amount we owe (usually a long-term debt for property) to someone (creditors). This long term liability is secured by mortgage property.

Failure on our part to pay or perform our promises, relating to the note, results in the creditor having the rights to go after certain assets (home, building, etc.).

(For comparison see notes receivable)

Direct Reduction
Mortgage Note

$18,000   Account No. <u>10</u>
                                            <u>December 10</u> 199X

For value received we jointly and severally, promise to pay to

<u>Barbara Bresnaan</u>

or order the sum of eighteen thousand dollars in or within 20 years from this date, with interest thereon at the rate of 8 1/2 percent per annum, payable in monthly installments of $156.21 on the first day of each month hereafter, which payments shall first be applied to interest then due and the balance thereof remaining applied to principal; the interest to be computed monthly in advance on the unpaid balance, together with such fines on interest in areas as are provided.

With the right to make additional payments on account of said principal sum on any payment date.

Failure to pay any of said installments within thirty (30) days from the date when the same becomes due, notwithstanding any license or waiver of any prior breach of conditions, shall make the whole of the balance of said principal sum immediately due and payable at the option of the holder thereof.

The makers, endorsers, and guarantors or other parties to this note, and each of the, severally waive demand, notice and protest.

Signed and sealed in the presence of

---

*See promissory note.

NEGOTIABLE INSTRUMENT

A legal document which usually can change title (rights of ownership) quickly.

This selling or transferring is usually done by signing the document or sometimes by just delivering it.

A promissory note usually is a negotiable instrument.

(See promissory note)

Negotiable Instrument

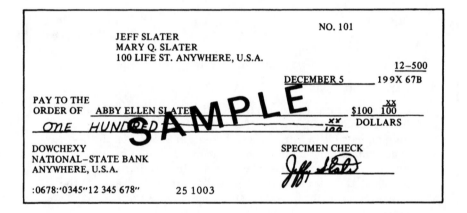

NET INCOME (NET PROFIT)

Amount that earned revenues exceed incurred expenses for a specific period of time.

Sales* (revenue) minus expenses = net income (or profit)

(See matching or operating statement)

Revenues (earned)
− Expenses (incurred)
= Net Income

*Earned revenue—incurred expenses. For a merchandise company see p. 110.

NET LOSS

Amount that incurred expenses exceed earned revenue for a specific period of time.

(See matching or operating statements)

Sales	$500,000
− Expenses	600,000
Net Loss	($100,000)

Service Company	Merchandise. Company
Sales	Sales
− Expenses	− Cogs
	= Gross Profit
= Net Income or Net Loss	− Operating Expenses
	= Net Income or Net Loss

NET PAY

The amount of money taken home by a worker from a business (or employer) in wages after all deductions (taxes, social security, etc.) are taken out.

(For comparison see gross pay)

	Gross Pay
–	Social Security
–	Medicare
–	FIT
–	SIT
–	Medical
–	Union
=	Net Pay

NET SALES

The total revenue(cashes well as charge sales) to a business from its operation minus any sales discounts and/or sales returns and allowances that the business gives or issues to its customers for a specific period of time.

(See gross sales)

Net Sales
Jim's Supermarket
Income Statement
for Year Ended December 31, 200X

Revenue from sales (gross sales)		$7,000,000
Less: Sales discounts	$500,000	
Sales returns and allowances	800,000	1,300,000
Net sales		$5,700,000

(See gross sales for comparison)

NOMINAL ACCOUNTS (TEMPORARY ACCOUNTS)

All revenue, costs and expenses, drawing, as well as income summary accounts.

Balances *of each account are* not carried over *to the next accounting period.*

Their balances are eventually summarized in order to determine a new figure *for capital (owner's equity) to* start *the* next *accounting period.*

(See closing entries for more detail, chart at end of book)

Nominal Accounts

Sales

Sales returns and allowance

Sale discounts

Purchases

Purchase return and allowance

Purchase discount

Income summary

Withdrawals

Salary expense

Rent expense

Advertising expense

Freight-in

(any revenue, expense, cost are temporary)

NON CUMULATIVE PREFERRED STOCK

A type of stock which usually gives to the investor a definite or certain amount of dividends each year.

If, for some reason, the dividends are not paid (in arrears) that year, or in the past years, the holders of non cumulative preferred stock are not *entitled to the past dividends when current dividends are paid.*

(See cumulative preferred stock)

Non cumulative Preferred Stock

Barry Katz bought 100 shares of non cumulative preferred stock of Moore Corporation through his local home town stockbroker.

The stockbroker had told Barry that this type of stock *will pay* him a $100 dividend per year.

However, if the company, for some reason, cannot pay a dividend (is in arrears), Barry *will not have rights* to the past unpaid dividends when present or future dividends are paid.

(See cumulative preferred stock for comparison)

NONPARTICIPATING PREFERRED STOCK

A type of stock which usually gives to the investor a definite or fixed amount of dividends from the corporation.

There is no opportunity for the preferred stockholders to "participate" or share in more or additional dividends that year.

Most preferred stock is nonparticipating.

(See cumulative preferred stock for further help)

Nonparticipating Preferred Stock

Facts: (Relating to Bobreck company)

1. There are 1,000 shares of preferred non participating stock outstanding
2. There are 5,000 shares of common stock outstanding (issued).
3. Holders of preferred stock get $1.00 per share each year (not allowed to join with common stockholders if more dividends are available).
4. Common stockholders get what is left after paying off the preferred stockholders.

Situation: A look at Bobreck for 1999 and 2000 relating to dividends

	1999	1999 Dividend Share	2000	2000 Dividend Share
Total dividends* to be paid	$1,000		$11,000	
To preferred	$1,000 (1,000 shr. X $1.00)	$1.00 $1,000 1,000 shrs.	$1,000 (1,000 shrs. X $1.00)	$1.00 ($1,000) 1,000 shr.
To common	0	0	$10,000 (5,000 shrs. X $2.00)	$2.00 ($10,000) 5,000 shr.

*based on company earnings

(See cumulative preferred for other possibilities)

NORMAL BALANCE—ACCOUNT

The normal balance is the side which is increased by the rules of debit and credit of an account.

Normal Balance

assets	debit
liabilities	credit
capital (owners' equity)	credit
drawing	debit
expenses	debit
revenue	credit
retained earnings	credit

(for specified titles see credit chart at end of book)

If cash (an asset) has a credit balance, what would it mean? We have overdrawn our checkbook, because we have a negative balance in cash. This situation would not be the normal balance of cash.

NOTES PAYABLE

The amount of the company owe someone (creditors). Because the company made a definite written promise which states that we will pay to the order of someone (payee) a certain amount of money at a certain date. Notes payable is a liability on the balance sheet.

(For opposite side of coin, see notes receivable)

Notes payable is a liability on the balance sheet.

NOTES RECEIVABLE

Someone owes us money and we have a written promise which states when we will receive a certain amount of money by a given date in the future. Notes receivable is an asset in the balance sheet.*

(See accounts receivable for comparison/or notes payable)

*notes receivable discounted is a contra asset account which shows the contingent liability for customers' notes that have been discounted.

ON ACCOUNT

To charge it. Buy now, pay later!

(see accounts payable)

OPPORTUNITY COST

The monetasry difference that could have been obtained between a decision made and an alternative decision.

THE DOT. COM COMPANY STOCK JUST TRIPLED! WE SHOULD HAVE INVESTED IN THAT— INSTEAD OF THE 'VEGGIE-FAST FOOD' RESTAURANT CHAIN!!

ORGANIZATION COSTS

The cost or expenditure which results from organizing a new company.

The total of all the costs are considered to be an intangible *asset called organization costs.*

Organization Costs

January 5: Enid Silberstein spent $1,000 for printing up stock certificates, paying legal fees, as well as paying the cost of getting a state charted in order to form Messier Corporation. The following entry was recorded by Messier Corporation:

Journal   Page #1

Date		Description (Accounts)	Folio (PR)	Debit	Credit
200X Jan.	5	Organization Cost	10	1,000	
		Cash	1		1,000

At the end of the first year, a portion of the balance sheet of Messier Corporation looked as follows:

Assets:

Current Assets: _____

_____

_____

_____

Plant Assets:

_____

_____

_____

Intangible Assets:

Organization costs	$1,000
Goodwill	500
Total Assets:	

OUTSTANDING CHECKS (CHECKS IN TRANSIT)

Checks written by a person or company that have not been received, or processed (or cleared) by the bank.

This would be subtracted from the bank balance in the preparation of a bank reconciliation.

(See bank reconciliation)

OVERAPPLIED OVERHEAD

The situation where more overhead was transferred to work in process than estimated or incurred. The balance of the account is a credit.

OWNER'S EQUITY

The share of a business that the owner has which is equaled to the company's assets less the liabilities

$$\begin{aligned} & Assets \\ - \ & Liabilities \\ \hline = \ & Owner's\ Eqiuity \end{aligned}$$

PAID-IN CAPITAL (CONTRIBUTED CAPITAL)

A section of stockholders' equity which shows:

1. Amount of stock a corporation has issued (or sold)

2. The premiums or discounts that have resulted from selling stock

3. The sale of treasury stock*

4. Stock received form donations

Stockholders' Equity = Paid -in capital + retained earnings

Paid-in Capital (Contributed Capital)
Stockholders' Equity (stockholders' investment)
Paid-in capital:
(contributed capital

Common stock	$400,000	
($10 par 40,000 shares issued		
Premium on common stock**	80,000	$480,000
(stock was sold at $12 per share or		
a $2 premium per share)		
From sale of treasury stock		10,000
Total paid-in capital (contributed)		$490,000

*See treasury stock.
**Many texts use titles such as paid-in capital in excess of par value-common stock

PAID-IN-CAPITAL-TREASURY-STOCK

A stockholders' equity account which is debited when treasury stock is sold at less than cost. The account is credited if sold for more than cost.

Facts: cost of treasury stock $50
    resold the treasury stock for $40
    paid-in-capital account — treasury stock will be debited for $10 along with a debit to cash for $40 and a credit to treasury stock for $50

PAR VALUE

A dollar value which is assigned to a share of stock arbitrarily (or at random).

Each state has its own regulations whether a corporation needs to assign a par value or not.

Why use par?

Par value is sometimes used to protect the creditors.

Some state laws require a corporation to keep a certain amount of the stockholders' investment in the business for the protection of the creditors. (This is called legal capital.)

Par value may be used in calculating legal capital.

(See minimum legal capital)

PARTICIPATING PREFERRED STOCK

A type of stock which usually gives to the investor a definite or certain amount of dividends (from the corporation) each year with the opportunity of the preferred stockholder to "participate" or share in more or additional dividends.

(See cumulative preferred stock for further help)

Participating Preferred Stock

Facts: (Relating to Bobreck Company)

1. There are 1,000 shares of preferred (participating) stock outstanding (issued).
2. There are 5,000 shares of common stock outstanding.
3. Holders of preferred stock get at least $1.00 per share each year.
4. Common stockholders get up to $1.00 per share before having to split with preferred (see No. 5).

153

5. Whatever is left (after common and preferred have been paid) or available to be paid out in dividends is split one-sixth to preferred and five-sixths to common (these are the rules of Bobreck).

Situation: A look at Bobreck for 1998 and 1999 relating to dividends:

	1998	1998 Dividend Share	1999	
Total dividends* to be paid	$1,000	✕	$12,000	✕
To preferred	$1,000 (1,000 shr. X $1.00)	$1.00 $1,000 1,000 shrs.	$2,000 $1,000 + 1,000 (1/6 X $6,000)	$2.00 ($2,000) 1,000 shr.
To common	0	0	$10,000 $5,000 + 5,000 (5/6 X $6,000)	$2.00 ($10,000) 5,000 shr.

*Based on a company's earnings

(See cumulative preferred for other possibilities)

PARTNERSHIP

A business owned by two or more people. (How the ownership is divided should be spelled out in a legal contract to avoid disputes later on.)

(See liquidation, or realization)

Partnership

Characteristics: Unlimited liability
Ease of formation
Limited life
Mutual agency

PATENTS (INTANGIBLE ASSETS)

An exclusive right for 17 years, which is granted by the federal government which allows one to sell, use, or manufacture a certain type of product.

Patents

Morris Blue, a retired shoe worker, invented a new type of car which uses air for fuel instead of gas.

Morris applied for a patent which the federal government. If granted Morris would have the exclusive right to manufacture the car.

PAYABLE

Means to owe. It is a liability. A payable account is a liability.

(See on account)

Payable

Jim bought a television form Cotoia, Inc.

He charged it for $100. Cotoia called Jim an account receivable, and Jim called Cotoia, Inc. an accounts payable (or he owed Cotoia, Inc. money).

PAYEE (PROMISSORY NOTE)

The person or company who will receive *money (check) from a promissory note (a definite written promise to pay as [payee] a definite sum of money at a fixed future date). The person or company making this promise is the maker.*

(See note receivable for further help)
(See maker for comparison)

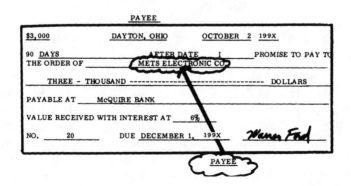

PAYROLL

*The total amount of wages or salaries which are paid to workers of a business for a specific period of time.**

(See payroll register, net pay, gross pay, FICA)

Payroll is based upon a calendar year which is broken into four quarters.

Quarter 1	Quarter 2	Quarter 3	Quarter 4
January	April	July	October
February	May	August	November
March	June	September	December

*Payroll is based on a calendar year for tax purposed.

PAYROLL REGISTER

A form (many columns) which contains and summarizes information about payroll (amount of money paid to workers less deductions) which is needed at the end of each payroll period.*

The payroll register may be used as a supplementary record or as a special journal.

(See employer's payroll taxes)

PAYROLL REGISTER

Employee Name	Allowances and Marital Status	Cumulative Earnings	Salary per Week	No. of Hrs.	Wages per Hour	Earnings			Cumulative Earnings	Taxable Earnings		
						Regular	Overtime	Gross		Federal Unemploy-ment	Soc. Sec.	Medicare
Jones, Bob	S-0	6800 00	—	39	16 00	624 00		624 00	7424 00	2000 00	624 00	624 00
King, Abby	S-1	6600 00	—	44	14 00	560 00	84 00	644 00	7244 00	4000 00	644 00	644 00
O'Mally, Susan	M-3	6462 500	1375 00			1375 00		1375 00	66000 00	—	775 00	1375 00
Regan, Pat	M-1	4230 000	900 00			900 00		900 00	43200 00	—	900 00	900 00
Zott, Jim	M-2	6486 000	1380 00			1380 00		1380 00	66240 00	—	540 00	1380 00
TOTALS		18518 500	3655 00			4839 00	84 00	4923 00	190108 00	6000 00	3483 00	4923 00

PAYROLL REGISTER

Deductions					Net Pay	Check No.	Distribution of Expense Accounts	
FICA		Federal Income Tax	State Income Tax	Medical Insurance			Office Salaries Expense	Market Wages Expense
Soc. Sec.	Medicare							
38 69	9 05	107 00	31 20	22 00	416 06	840		624 00
39 93	9 34	100 00	32 20	22 00	440 53	841		644 00
48 05	19 94	222 00	68 75	44 00	972 26	842	1375 00	
55 80	13 05	117 00	45 00	44 00	625 15	843	900 00	
33 48	20 01	238 00	69 00	44 00	975 51	844	1380 00	
215 95	71 39	784 00	246 15	176 00	3429 51		3655 00	1268 00

*Payroll is based on a calendar year for tax purposes.

PENCIL FOOTING

Summarizing the debits (left side of any account) and credits (right side of any account) of an account to get a new balance.

Pencil Footing

	Cash	
100		200
500		50
500		60
800		*310*
490		

The side which has the largest amount of balance ($800) is not moved, while the smaller side ($310) is brought over and subtracted. The new balance ($490) remains on the side which had the largest amount or balance.

PERIODIC INVENTORY SYSTEM

An inventory system which does not try at the time of each sale of merchandise (good) to calculate the cost *of each "good" that is sold by the company.*

In this system one waits until the end of an accounting period to determine at one time the cost of all goods (merchandise) *sold by the company during this period.*

(See perpetual inventory for comparison)

(For calculating a cost of ending inventory, see FIFO, LIFO, weighted average, gross profit method and retail method)

It is the merchandise inventory account which shows the

beginning inventory. It is the purchase account which records the cost of additional purchases. At end of period a physical count of inventory is taken to determine the cost of goods sold.

PERPETUAL INVENTORY SYSTEM

An inventory system which keeps continual *track of how much inventory (merchandise, goods) is on hand.*

This system usually uses forms (cards) that keep track of the number of amount of each good received or sold.

Usually once a year physical count is taken to verify the records.

Today with computers, the perpetual inventory system is used quite often.

(See periodic inventory for comparison)

INVENTORY CONTROL

Part No. _____

Description _____   Maximum _____

Prime Supplier _____   Reorder Level _____

Location _____   Reorder Quantity _____

Date	Received			Sold			Balance		
	Units	Cost/Unit	Total	Units	Cost/Unit	Total	Units	Cost/Unit	Total
200X July 1	Balance Fwd.						8	$60	$240
4	20	64	$680				8	60	
							20	64	880
				8	$60	$240			
				8	64	256			
7							12	64	384

Key Points:
1. Balance of inventory account continually updated.
2. At time of sale cogs is recorded.
3. A purchase account is not used.

PETTY CASH FUND

A sum of money that is set aside (in a fund) that allows a company to pay cash for its small bills or obligations instead of having to write a check (this is usually done with vouchers).

Cash in fund plus vouchers in fund covering payments must equal original balance in petty cash.

(See example of illustrating a voucher)

Petty Cash Voucher

	Voucher Number __658__
	Date __5/31/00__

Paid to __Gants__

Purpose __supplies__

(Attach supporting documents below)

Gants				
Nov-2	8 1 3			
	$	0.25GrA	Balance carried forward	$31.83
	$	0.25GrA	This expenditure	.77
	$	0.25GrA		
	$	0.02TxA	Balance	31.06
	*$	0.77TlA	Amount replenished	18.94
			Balance	$50.00

Use only when replenishment is made.

Most petty cash vouchers show only specific payments with no running balance.

The establishment of petty cash results in a debit to petty cash and a credit to cash.

The payments out of petty cash are recorded in the auxiliary petty cash record—it is at time of replenishment that the individual expenses will be debited and a cover check written to replenish petty cash.

The only time petty cash is debited would be to raise it to a new level.

A petty cash voucher shows the amount and reason for each cash payment.

POST-CLOSING TRIAL BALANCE (POST-CLEARING TRIAL BALANCE)

A trial balance (list of the ledger) which is taken after *the adjusting and closing entries have been posted to the ledger.*

The post-closing trial balance should contain only *permanent accounts (assets, liabilities, and one new figure for capital). All temporary accounts (revenue, expense, drawing, as well as income summary) have* zero *balances.* They do not appear on the post-closing trial balance.

Once again, the post-closing trial balance shows equality of debits and credits in the ledger.

Joe's Market
Post-Closing Trial Balance
for Year Ended December 31, 200X

	Debit	Credit
Cash	1,000	
Accounts receivable	500	
Merchandise inventory	200	
Equipment	100	
Accumulated depreciation, equipment		50
Accounts payable		450
J. Smith, capital		1,300
	1,800	1,800

Key Point: By journalizing and posting the closing entries to the ledger, all temporary accounts have a zero balance and this information has been summarized in J. Smith, capital.

POST-REFERENCE (FOLIO) (ACCOUNT NUMBER)

A. In a journal, a column which shows the number of the account to which information has been transferred (posted) to the ledger.

B. In a ledger, a column which shows the number of the journal page from which a posting or transfer of information has come.

Post Reference (Folio)

General Journal   Page #5

Date		Description (accounts)	Folio (PR)	Debit	Credit
200X Nov.	1	Cash	12	500	
		Sales	4		500
		(Cash sales for the day)			

Ledger

Cash

Account No. 12

Date	Explanation	Folio (PR)	Debit	Date	Explanation	Folio (PR	Credit
200X Nov. 1		GJ 5	500				

Sales

Account No. 4

Date	Explanation	Folio (PR)	Debit	Date	Explanation	Folio (PR	Credit
				199X Nov. 1		GJ 5	500

Key Point: PR numbers should never be recorded until posting is finished. One purpose of PR numbers is to indicate whether or not posting has been completed.

PREDETERMINED OVERHEAD RATE

The expected or planned normal overhead cost, often determined over a long enough time period to avoid seasonal flucuations.

PREEMPTIVE RIGHT

The stockholders in a corporation have the right to buy additional *(or more) shares of stock when the corporation sells new shares of stock.*

The stockholder would buy more stock in order to keep his same fractional amount, *(or proportional)* interest *or* rights *in the corporation.*

Preemptive Right

Jim Tabbut owns 25% of all the common stock issued by AV Laboratories.

On January 5, AV Laboratories announced an intent to sell an additional 100,000 new shares of common stock.

Jim called the company because he was concerned about losing his 25% interest in the company.

The company assured Jim that under preemptive rights he would be given the option to buy 25,000 shares of the new issue if he wanted, although he surely would not be forced into buying the new stock.

PREFERRED STOCK

To the investor:

A type of stock which shows the amount of ownership and the rights one has in a corporation.

This type of stock usually gives the investors certain special privileged rights as to how they may share in the profits or earnings of a corporation during the year.

To a corporation:

This usually means a way of raising money (from a wider variety of investors) by selling shares of preferred stock to investors.

Some investors who do not like common stock may *invest in preferred stock.*

(See common stock)

PREMIUM ON STOCK (CAPITAL CONTRIBUTED IN EXCESS OF PAR)

The result of selling stock (or issuing stock) at a price that is greater than par value.

(See par value for further help, discount on stock)

Premium on Stock

On July 1, the Blance Corporation issued 500 shares, $10 par common stock at $12 per share.

The following entry was made on the company's books:

Journal   Page #1

Date		Description (Accounts)	Folio (PR)	Debit	Credit
200X July	1	Cash	1	6,000	
		Common stock	10		5,000*
		Premium on common stock	11		1,000

*(500 shares x $10 par)

(See discount on stock for comparison)

Key Point: Premium on common stock is a capital account on the corporate balance sheet with a normal balance of a credit.

166

PREPAID EXPENSES

Expenses that have been paid for ahead of time. When you get them, they are recorded assets; when you use them up, they are assigned as expenses. Prepaid expenses are located on the balance sheet with a debit balance.

Prepaid Expenses

Ed Sloan opened up a dress shop, but his landlord, not trusting him, demanded that Ed pay three months' rent in advance.

The transaction was recorded as follows:

		Journal			Page #1
Date		**Description (Accounts)**	**Folio (PR)**	**Debit**	**Credit**
200X Jan.	1	Prepaid rent	5	XXXX	
		Cash	1		XXXX

PREPAID RENT

Paying ahead of time for rent which has not been used up yet. When it gets used up, it will be an expense, but for now it is an asset (property or thing of value owned by the business).

Prepaid Rent

John Mills paid three months' rent, $900, in advance to Texas Real Estate. At the end of the first month, the asset prepaid rent now had a balance of $600, since $300 was now recorded as rent expense.

PRICE-EARNINGS RATIO

The current market price of a stock divided by the earnings per share.

OUR STOCK IS NOW $48.00 PER SHARE. EARNINGS ARE $4.00 PER SHARE. OUR PRICE-EARNINGS RATIO IS 12!

PRINCIPLE OF CONSERVATISM

A guideline or rule which, in the past, tended to emphasize that a company should not be too optimistic in valuing certain accounts, but should take a more conservative view (which would reduce net income or lessen an asset's value).

This principle looked ahead to the possibilities of a company not having profit and therefore having to provide for its losses (a very conservative attitude).

The attitude toward this principle is changing, and concepts of materiality, objectivity and consistency, etc., are being considered before the principle of conservatism, although conservatism is still a consideration.

PRINCIPLE OF CONSISTENCY

A business may use many different accounting rules or guidelines to prepare its income and balance sheet statements in an attempt to reflect net income fairly.

In order for a person to compare a company's statements from year to year (to see trends or how a company is doing), one must be sure the company is using the same accounting principles (or is being consistent) each year to prepare those statements.

Principle of Consistency

With inflation, Jones Corporation changed from FIFO to LIFO, the result being less profit and also having fewer taxes to pay. The editor of a local paper questions if the principle of consistency was being followed in the best interest of the public.

PRINCIPLE OF MATERIALITY

Instances when a business doesn't have to strictly follow certain accounting principles:

1. The cost of implementing that principle is excessive (or prohibitive) to follow, and

2. The business financial statement will not be greatly affected.

To decide about materiality is often a "judgement decision."

Principle of Materiality

James Corporation bought a desk lamp for 40 dollars.

The company felt that they should record the cost of the lamp as an expense (instead of an asset) because it would cost more (to the company) to depreciate it over five years, and the result of recording it as an expense would not materially affect the outcome of James' financial statements.

PRINCIPLE OF OBJECTIVITY

When a business performs the accounting cycle (recording transactions, preparing statements, etc.), it must be able to back up (or verify) factually the figures or data that have been used. This is done by a company keeping copies of its records (bills, bank statements, purchase orders, etc.).

If records are not available, a company may have to show the logic or sound judgement that was used (maybe how an estimate for bad debts was made) to arrive at a certain figure.

PRIVATE ACCOUNTANT

A worker (employee) who is doing accounting for a company. He works only for that company.

(See public accountant)

Private Accountant

Francis Manning opened up a hot dog and milk stand. The operation became so big that Frank hired a full-time person to handle the accounting.

PROCESS COST-ACCOUNTING

A perpetual inventory accounting system that accumulates costs according to a specific department's process in the firm.

PROMISSORY NOTE

A promise in writing to pay a definite amount of money at a certain date (as agreed upon in the agreement) signed by the maker.

(See maker for detail, mortgage note payable)

PROTEST NOTICE

A written statement by a bank which tells of the failure of someone (the maker) to pay his note or written promise when it came due (maturity).

This statement is sent to the person who is contingently liable (now responsible to pay for the note or promise to the bank because the other person [maker] failed to pay).

(See contingent liability for more detail)

Protest Notice

On June 2, the Blue Bank notified Jim Driscoll that he must pay a note receivable that was dishonored by Joe Walker. Why?

This is the way it happened:

On January 1, Jim Driscoll decided he couldn't wait for the money and discounted the note at the Blue Bank, with a stipulation that, if Joe Walker didn't pay off his promise on June 1, he would pay it to the bank (Jim being contingently liable).

Well, on June 1, Joe Walker never paid, so the bank sent a *protest notice* to Jim Driscoll.

PUBLIC ACCOUNTANT

A person who provides an accounting service (or function) to the general public for a certain fee.

(See private accountant)

Public Accountant

Ed Monroe just opened up a small health lounge. He really didn't understand how to set up an accounting system; therefore, he called in a public accounting firm to act as consultants. Ed's business *never* grew so big that it *required* a full-time accountant.

PURCHASES ACCOUNT

An account which shows or accumulates the amount of merchandise (goods) bought or purchased for resale to one's customers during the current accounting period.

Purchase has a debit balance and is also found on the income statement as a cost of goods sold.

(See purchase discounts/or purchase, returns and allowances)

On January 4, the B and L Supermarket bought $5,000 worth of merchandise (goods or purchases for resale to its customers) on account from Keeney Food Wholesalers.
The B and L Supermarket made the following transaction to record the purchase: ⌐

Journal   Page #1

Date		Description (Accounts)	Folio (PR)	Debit	Credit
200X Jan.	4	Purchases	5	5,000	
		Accounts payable—	8		5,000
		Keeney Food Wholesaler			

(See cost of goods sold for more information)

174

PURCHASE DISCOUNTS ACCOUNT

An account which shows the savings or reduction of costs by a company that pays for merchandise before a discount date set by the seller. Purchase discount balance found on the income statement has a credit balance.

(See purchase account, purchase returns and allowances)

Jan. 5 Moe Glass Inc. bought $300 worth of purchases (merchandise for resale) from Jim's Wholesale Lobster Company. Terms of sale were 2/10, N/30 (if Moe paid the bill within 10 days, he receives 2% or $6 off the Bill). The following entry was recorded:

Journal   Page #1

Date		Description (Accounts)	Folio (PR)	Debit	Credit
199X					
Jan.	5	Purchases	10	300	
		Accounts payable—Jim	12		300

Jan. 8 Moe Glass pays the bill. The following entry was recorded:

Journal   Page #2

Date		Description (Accounts)	Folio (PR)	Debit	Credit
199X					
Jan.	8	Accounts payable	12	300	
		Purchase discount	11		6
		Cash	1		294

(See sales discount for comparison)

Key Point: Purchase discount is a temporary account that is categorized as a contra cost of goods sold. Account used in a periodic system.

PURCHASE JOURNAL

A book or place (special journal) where transactions are recorded when buying something (purchase, supplies, etc.) on account (buy now, pay later).

Purchase Journal

Transactions:

Dec. 3 Bought merchandise on account from J.P. Shoes $3,000.

Dec. 5 Bought store supplies on account, $200, from V-Supplies.

Dec. 8 Bought a car on account, $5,000, from T.T. Used Cars.

Purchase Journal

Date	Accounts Credited	Folio (PR)	Accounts Payable Credit	Purchase Debit	Store Supplies Debit	Account Fol. Am't (PR)		
200X								
Dec. 3	J.P. Shoes	√	3,000	3,000				
5	V-Supplies	√	200		200			
8	T.T. used crs.	√	5,000			equip.	215	5,000
	Total		8,200		200			5,000
			(211)	(510)	(281)			√

Accounts Payable
During the month post to J.P. Shoes, V-Supplies, and T.T. Used Cars in the A/P subsidiary ledger as credits. When this is done, checks ✓ are placed in the post reference column.

The total ($8,200) is posted too, as a credit to A/P account #211 in the general ledger at the end of the month.

Purchases
The total of the column is posted at *the end of the month* to purchases account number 510 in the general ledger.

Store Supplies
The total of this column is posted at *the end of the month* to store supplies account #281 in the general ledger.

The total of this column is never posted. A check ✓ is placed to show this.

A debit to equipment (account #215) is posted to the general ledger *any time during the month.*

PURCHASE ORDER

A form used by the purchasing department to order some goods or merchandise from a supplier requesting the items be shipped to the purchaser.

Purchase Order

7451174	End, Inc. P.O. Box 10 26 Sable Road Salem, Ma 01945

P.O. Number

This number must appear on all shipping labels, invoice packing slips and B/L.

TO: ⌐   ⌐

SHIP TO: ⌐

L   L   L

Date of Order	Date Needed	Ship Via	FOB
Terms	For Resale	For Own Use	Dept. or Req. No.	Ac't #

Quotation No.

Quantity		Please Supply Items Listed Below	Price	Amount
Ordered	Received			

In consideration of end entering into this agreement with __vendor__ , __vendor__ warrants that all goods sold hereunder shall not contain hazardous substances, as defined under the provisions of the federal hazardous substances act and the regulations issued thereunder, and __vendor__ agrees to indemnify and hold harmless from any breach of this warranty.

Authorized by _____

A purchase requisition is a written request within the company indicating the need to create a purchase order.

PURCHASES RETURNS AND ALLOWANCES ACCOUNT

An account which shows the amount of merchandise (goods) returned to suppliers for a price reduction allowed by suppliers for defective or returned goods in a periodic inventory system.

(See purchase discounts)

Purchases returns and allowances

On Jan. 5, Moe Glass Inc. bought $300 worth of lobsters (purchased for resale) on account from Jim's Wholesale Lobster Company.

On Jan. 6, Moe Glass issued a debit memo (reducing what they owed Jim's Wholesale) and returned $100 worth of lobsters to Jim's Wholesale because these lobsters were diseased.

Moe made the following entry:

| | Journal | | Page #1 | | |
Date		Description (Accounts)	Folio (PR)	Debit	Credit
200X Jan.	6	Accounts payable— Jim's whls. lobs.	10	100	
		Purchases returns and allow.	12		100

QUICK ASSETS (LIQUID ASSETS)

Something (asset) a business owns that is very close to being considered as good as cash (if that asset has to be turned into cash) for some need of the business.

Quick Assets (Liquid Assets)

Cash

Notes Receivable

Accounts Receivable

Marketable Securities

RATE OF RETURN ON ASSETS

Net income (profit divided by total assets [current and long-term]) which give us an indication of how profitable the business was, compared to the amount of assets invested in the business.*

Rate of return on assets helps to answer the question of how efficiently the company used its assets.

Rate of Return on Assets

1.	Net income after taxes	19,000
2.	Add interest costs	1,000
3.	Net income before interest costs	20,000
4.	Total assets at start of the year	400,000
5.	Total assets at end of the year	500,000
6.	Average of assets used	450,000

$$\text{Rate of return on assets used} = \frac{\text{Line 3}}{\text{Line 6}} = \frac{\$20,000}{\$450,000} = 4.4\%$$

Is it good or bad?

One must check previous years' ratios of the company as well as ratios of other companies in the same type of industry in order to come up with some type of meaningful analysis.

---

* See example if you want to use average total of assets.

RATE OF RETURN ON STOCKHOLDERS' EQUITY

Net income (profit) divided by stockholders' equity.*

This measures how productive the owner's equity was.

Rate of Return on Stockholders' Equity

1. Net income after taxes	$100,000
2. Common stockholders' equity, start of year	200,000
3. Common stockholders' equity, end of year	300,000
4. Average common stockholders' equity	250,000

Rate of return on common stockholders' equity:

$$\frac{\text{(Line 1)}}{\text{(Line 4)}} \quad \frac{\$100,000}{250,000} = 40\%$$

One must check previous years' ratios of the company, as well as ratios of other companies in the same type of industry, in order to come up with some type of meaningful analysis.

*(See stockholder's equity)

RAW MATERIALS INVENTORY

Those goods used in the manufacturing of a product. These goods, classified as an asset, on the balance sheet.

REAL ACCOUNTS (PERMANENT)

Assets, liabilities, and capital (owner's equity). Each ending balance is carried over to the next accounting period.

(See nominal accounts)

Real Accounts (Permanent)

Assets	Liabilities	Owner's Equity (stockholder's equity)
Cash	Accounts payable	Capital (owner's equity)
Supplies	Notes payable	Common stock
Prepaid rent	Mortgage payable	Retained earnings
Equipment	Dividends payable	

Temporary Accounts

All revenues, expenses, income summary and drawing.

REALIZATION — PARTNERSHIP

The amount of money that is received (or realized) in selling assets *during the "winding-up process" by a company that is going out of business.*

(See liquidation)

Carolyn Bergstrom Hair Stylists
Before Liquidation

Cash	$10,000	
All noncash assets	60,000	
All liabilities		$10,000
T. Duffy, capital		20,000
C. Bergstrom, capital		20,000
C. Peterson, capital		20,000
Total	$70,000	$70,000

Sold all noncash assets for $90,000, showing a gain in realization of $30,000.

The entries to record the several steps in the liquidation process as follows:

Journal   Page #1

Date		Description (Accounts)	Folio (PR)	Debit	Credit
200X Jan.	1	Cash		90,000	
		Assets			60,000
		Gain on realization			30,000

Journal   Page #1

Date		Description (Accounts)	Folio (PR)	Debit	Credit
200X Jan.	1	Gain on realization		30,000	
		T. Duffy, capital			10,000
		C. Bergstrom, capital			10,000
		C. Peterson, capital			10,000

After Realization

Cash	$100,000	
All liabilities		$ 10,000
T. Duffy, capital		30,000
C. Bergstrom, capital	30,000	
C. Peterson, capital		30,000
Total	$100,000	$100,000

(All noncash assets off books)

REGISTERED BONDS

The company issuing registered bonds keeps an up-to-date *record of the names and addresses of each bond holder.*

The bond can be transferred from one to another; therefore, the company keeps track of the bond owner (or new owners), which results in fewer *problems of theft or loss.*

Payments of interest are then sent to the owner of record.

Registered Bonds

John Driscoll, owner of a registered bond, transferred ownership of his bond to Pete Williams (by signing over the bond).

Pete Williams failed to notify the company, and the interest payment by the company was sent to John Driscoll. Needless to say, adjustments were made to transfer the interest payment to Pete, as well as officially get Pete Williams' name on the records of the company (for payments in the future).

RESIDUAL VALUE

A portion of the cost *of a plant asset (equipment) that one expects to get back when it is removed or has reached the end of its productive life.*

Residual value is hard to estimate but gives us an estimate of how much depreciation should be taken for a plant asset (equipment) over its lifetime.

Equipment – residual value = amount of depreciation to be taken over the lifetime of a plant asset.

Residual Value

Warren Ford bought a new truck for his sales fleet for $25,000.

Based on guidelines set up by the Internal Revenue Service, as well as past history of his other vehicles, Warren estimated that in five years he could sell or trade the truck in the marketplace for $3000.

Warren calculated he could depreciate the truck $22,000 over the next five years.

Truck	–	residual value	=	amount to be depreciated
$25,000		$3000		$22,000

184

RETAIL METHOD INVENTORY

A method used by a retail business to assign a cost or dollar figure for ending *inventory at the end of a period of time (month, three months, etc.) and thus estimate cost of goods sold.*

This method saves the business from having to physically count ending inventory each time *an income statement is wanted by management. A physical count of inventory should be done for the end-of-the-year statements.*

Retail Method Inventory

	Cost to Store	(Price to Customers) Retail Price
Beginning merchandise inventory	$10,000	$20,000
New purchases (less returns, etc.)	30,000	60,000
Cost of merchandise available to sell to the customers (at cost and retail)	$40,000	$80,000

$$\frac{Cost}{Retail} \quad \frac{\$40,000}{\$80,000} = 50\%$$

If sales for January 1 (net) =	$50,000
and ending inventory on January 31 at retail =	30,000
The cost of ending inventory on January 31 at cost =	15,000
(50% x $30,000)	

Steps:
1. Calculate cost to retail %.
2. Estimate the ending inventory at retail by deducting sales from the merchandise available for sale at retail.
3. Reduce the inventory at retail to cost.

Note: Retail companies sell goods to final consumers.

RETAINED EARNINGS

That portion or part of profits or earnings of a corporation that are kept or retained in the business which have been accumulating or building up in the business over the years.

If a corporation has a deficit (or loses money), it would reduce retained earnings.

The amount of retained earnings doesn't mean how much cash the business has.

(See deficit — retained earnings)

Retained Earnings
Stockholders' Equity (Shareholders' Equity)

Paid-In Capital:
(Contributed Capital)

Common Stock $100,000		Ret. Earnings (Jan. 1) $10,000
Retained Earnings 20,000		+ Net Income (Jan.) $10,000
		= Ret. Earnings (Jan. 31) $20,000
Total Stockholders' Equity $120,000		

RETAINED EARNINGS STATEMENT

A report or statement which shows the changes that have taken place *in retained earnings during an accounting period.*

Retained Earnings Statement
Metzner Co.
Retained Earnings Statement
for Year Ended December 31, 200X

Retained Earnings, Jan. 1, 200X		$10,000
Add: Net income per income statement	$6,000	
Collection of income tax refund	3,500	9,500
for prior years		$19,500
Deduct: Dividends declared on 500 shares	$ 500	
common stock		
Dividends declared on 1,000 shares	1,000	1,500
preferred stock		
Retained Earnings, December 31, 199X		$18,000

RETURN ON INVESTMENT

Profit or income as a percentage of invested assets. An indication of measurement of the ability of a company (or segment of a company) to utilize financial resources.

REVENUES

A subdivision of owners' equity which records the amount a company earns from sales of its products or services. The revenue results in an inward flow of assets.

(See matching concept)

Key Point: Revenue is not an asset. It is a temporary account with a normal balance of credit.
Earned revenue results in an inward flow of assets (cash and/or accounts receivable).

REVENUE EXPENDITURE

After a business buys a plant asset (truck), certain expenditures (costs) will result in order to keep the plant asset at its "full usefulness" as determined by the business.

If the expenditures (costs) only help to keep the plant asset at its full usefulness for the current accounting period, *this is called a* revenue expenditure.

(This expenditure is deducted from revenue on the year-end income statement as an expense.)

(See capital expenditure)

An expenditure of this nature is immediately expensed.

REVERSING ENTRY

A journal entry that reverses the effects of an adjusting entry. This entry is made the first day of the new accounting period.

(See accrued expenses)

Reversing Entry

Steps

    A. Go to "Accrued Expenses" and read about Jim Jackson to see an adjusting entry.

    B. Come back to this page to see how easy reversing entries really are.

    Do not go on until you have completed step A!!! Sorry for the inconvenience.

    Welcome back!

    Now let's see how:

    Jim will not *overstate* his expenses in the new year.

Key Point: Reversing entries may be used for only specific types of adjusting entries. These usually involve transactions of cash to be paid or received in the next accounting period.

See example on next page.

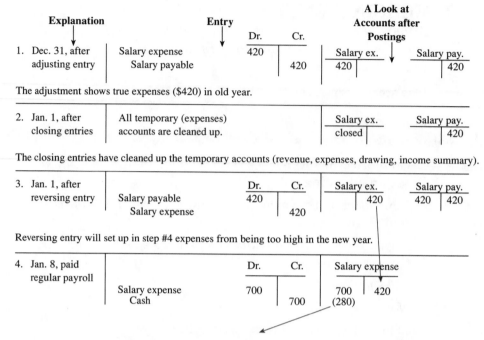

	Explanation	Entry	Dr.	Cr.	A Look at Accounts after Postings
1.	Dec. 31, after adjusting entry	Salary expense Salary payable	420	420	Salary ex. 420 | / Salary pay. | 420

The adjustment shows true expenses ($420) in old year.

| 2. | Jan. 1, after closing entries | All temporary (expenses) accounts are cleaned up. | | | Salary ex. closed \| / Salary pay. \| 420 |

The closing entries have cleaned up the temporary accounts (revenue, expenses, drawing, income summary).

			Dr.	Cr.	
3.	Jan. 1, after reversing entry	Salary payable Salary expense	420	420	Salary ex. | 420 / Salary pay. 420 | 420

Reversing entry will set up in step #4 expenses from being too high in the new year.

			Dr.	Cr.	
4.	Jan. 8, paid regular payroll	Salary expense Cash	700	700	Salary expense 700 | 420 (280)

True expense of new year ($280). It is the reversing entry that puts a credit into the salaries expense ($420) to reduce or give a true picture of the actual expense in the new year when the regular payroll is paid (January 8).

If $420 was omitted, (salary expense), it would appear all $700

700 |

of salaries is an expense in the new year. We know that a part of the $700 is an expense of the old year (as shown by the year-end adjusting entry).

Insight: The reversing entries allow the bookkeeper to proceed with the routine recording functions without having to recognize portions that were accrued.

RULES OF DEBITS AND CREDITS

Assets	=	Debit for increase, credit for decrease
Liabilities	=	Debit for decrease, credit for increase
Capital	=	Debit for decrease, credit for increase
Revenue	=	Debit for decrease, credit for increase
Expense	=	Debit for increase, credit for decrease
Drawing (withdrawal)	=	Debit for increase, credit for decrease

or

	Increase	Decrease	Normal Balance
Assets	debit	credit	debit
Liabilities	credit	debit	credit
Capital	credit	debit	credit
Revenue	credit	debit	credit
Expense	debit	credit	debit
Drawing	debit	credit	debit

(Both say same thing)

Analyzing Business Transactions
1. What accounts are affected?
2. Are they going up or down?
3. Are they assets, liabilities, etc.?
4. Is it a debit or credit?

Assets	+	Expenses	+	Withdrawal	=	Liabilities	+	Capital	+	Revenue
Dr. | Cr.		Dr. | Cr.		Dr. | Cr.		Dr. | Cr.		Dr. | Cr.		Dr. | Cr.
+ | −		+ | −		+ | −		− | +		− | +		− | +

SALARIES PAYABLE

We owe employees money for work they have done for us and have not been paid for yet. Salaries payable is a liability on the balance sheet.

(See accrued expenses)

Salaries Payable

Jim Brewer owns a minor league baseball team.

Business has been slow of late, and Jim has not been able to pay wages to his ballplayers for the last month. Jim has created salaries payable.

SALES DISCOUNT

A savings off the regular price of goods or services due to early payment of a bill by one's customers.

The sales discount (a debit balance) reduces the revenue (credit balance) a company collects and therefore reduces the total dollar amount of a company's sales. Sales discount is a contra revenue account found on the income statement.

(See sales returns and allowances)

Sales Discount

Jan. 5 Jim's Wholesale Lobster Co. sold on account $300 worth of lobsters to Moe Glass Inc. Terms of sale were 2/10, N/30. (If Moe Glass pays within 20 days, we [Jim's Wholesale] will give him a 2% reduction or $6 off the regular price.)

At the time of the sale, Jim's Wholesale made the following entry:

	Journal		Page #1	
Date	**Description (accounts)**	**Folio (PR)**	**Debit**	**Credit**
200X Jan. 5	Accounts rec.-Moe Glass	2	300	
	Sales	5		300

	Journal		Page #2	
Date	**Description (Accounts)**	**Folio (PR)**	**Debit**	**Credit**
200X Jan. 8	Cash	1	294	
	Sales discount	6	6	
	Accounts rec.-Moe Glass	2		300

(See purchase discount for comparison)

192

SALES JOURNAL

A book or place (special journal) where transactions are recorded only *when sales are made* on account *(haven't received cash yet).*

Sales Journal
200X

Sept. 1 Invoice 109 to Miller & Co., $100

    2 Sold merchandise on account to Mitchell and Mark Inc. ???
[new line?] invoice 633, for $2,000

Date		Invoice Number	Accounts Debited	Folio (PR)	Accounts Rec. Debit Sales Credit
200X Sept.	1	109	Miller and Co.	✓	100
	2	633	Mitchell and Mark	✓	2,000
			Totals		2,100
					(10) (20)

POSTING RULES

During the month, (daily) post to each individual account (Miller & Co., Mitchell & Mark) in the accounts receivable subsidiary ledger. A check ✓ is placed in the post reference column.

At the *end of the month* the total of $2,100 is posted to the general ledger as a *debit to accounts receivable* and credit to sales.

A/R   Sales

(Account Number 10)   (Account Number 20)

SALES RETURNS AND ALLOWANCES ACCOUNT

An account which shows the amount of merchandise or goods that a company or person (who isn't satisfied) returns or gets a partial allowance on price.

Sales have credit balances. Sales returns and allowances have debit balances or reduce the total sales of the company. Sales returns and allowances is a temporary contra revenue account found on the income statement.

(See sales discounts)

SALES RETURNS AND ALLOWANCES ACCOUNT

On January 5, Jim's Wholesale Lobster Co. sold on account $300 worth of lobsters to Moe Glass Inc.

On January 6, Moe Glass issued a debit memo (reducing what they owed Jim's Wholesale) and returned $100 worth of lobsters to Jim's Wholesale because these lobsters were diseased.

Jim's Wholesale made the following entry (credit memo):

Journal   Page #1

Date		Description (accounts)	Folio (PR)	Debit	Credit
200X Jan.	1	Sales returns and allowances	10	100	
		Accounts Receivable—M. Glass	5		100

(See debit or credit memo for back-up)

SALVAGE VALUE (SCRAP, RESIDUAL)

The amount of a plant asset (equipment) that one can get back (from estimating market value) when it is sold or at the end of its productive life.

Equipment – salvage value = amount of depreciation to be taken over the life of a plant asset.

Salvage Value

Warren Ford bought a new truck for his sales fleet for $25,000.

Based on guidelines set up by the Internal Revenue Service, as well as past history of his other vehicles, Warren estimated in five years he could sell or trade the truck in the marketplace for $3000.

Warren calculated he would depreciate the truck $22,000 over the next five years.

Truck	–	salvage value	=	amount to be depreciated
$25,000	–	$3000	=	$22,000

194

SCHEDULE OF ACCOUNTS PAYABLE

A list of individual *people or companies we owe money to (creditors).*

The total of this list should equal the one figure in accounts payable (controlling account) in the general ledger after postings at the end of a period.

(See schedule of accounts receivable)

Schedule of Accounts Payable

Accounts Payable Ledger
(Subsidiary)

Cough Brothers

Date		Item	Folio (PR)	Debit	Credit	Balance Debit	Credit
200X Dec.	1		PJ 1		200		200
	10		CD 1	200		--------	--------

Ralph Brothers

Date		Item	Folio (PR)	Debit	Credit	Balance Debit	Credit
200X April	1		PJ 1		500		500

Smith Brothers

Date		Item	Folio (PR)	Debit	Credit	Balance Debit	Credit
200X May	10		PJ 1		300		300

Cashman Company
Schedule of Accounts Payable
December 31, 200X

Ralph Brothers	$500
Smith Brothers	300
Total accounts payable	$800*

* This will be the balance in the accounts payable controlling account in the general ledger at the end of month.

SCHEDULE OF ACCOUNTS RECEIVABLE

A list of individual customers who owe us money. The total of the list should equal the one figure in accounts receivable (controlling accounts) in the general ledger after postings at the end of the period.

(See schedule of accounts payable)

Schedule of Accounts Receivable

Accounts Receivable Ledger*
(Subsidiary)

Bush and Bee Inc.

Date		Item	Folio (PR)	Debit	Credit	Balance Debit	Credit
200X May	1		SJ 1	300		300	
			CR 1		300	——	——

Miller and Company

Date		Item	Folio (PR)	Debit	Credit	Balance Debit	Credit
200X March	1		SJ 1	300		300	

Mitchell and Mark Inc.

Date		Item	Folio (PR)	Debit	Credit	Balance Debit	Credit
200X April	1		SJ 1	3,000		3,000	
			GJ 1		1,000	2,000	——

*Not found in general ledger.

Cashman Company
Schedule of Accounts Receivable
December 31, 200X

Miller and Co.	$ 300
Mitchell and Mark Inc.	2,000
Total accounts receivable	$2,300*

* This will be the balance in the accounts receivable controlling account in the general ledger at end of month.

196

SCRAP VALUE

A portion of the cost of a plant asset (equipment) that one can get back when it has reached the end of its productive life.

Scrap value is hard to estimate but it gives us an estimate of how much depreciation should be taken on a plant asset (equipment) over its lifetime.

Equipment – scrap value = amount of depreciation to be taken over the lifetime of the plan asset.

Scrap Value

Warren Ford bought a new truck for his sales fleet for $5,000.

Based on guidelines set up by the Internal Revenue Service, as well as past history of his other vehicles, Warren estimated in five years he could sell or trade the truck in the marketplace for $200.

Warren calculated he would depreciate the truck $4,800 over the next five years.

Truck	–	salvage value	=	amount to be depreciated
$5,000	–	$200	=	$4,800

SECURED BONDS

Bonds which are sold by a company that are backed up or secured by other specific asset(s) (buildings, equipment, etc.) of the company or other companies.

This becomes important if the company fails to pay off the bond when it comes due.

If this happens, the investor can go after what was secured on the bond.

Secured Bonds

Ron Hurley, holder of a secured bond, was quite concerned when the company failed to honor its obligation.

Ron went to his lawyer, who told him that the bond stated that in cases of nonpayment, the bond holder (Ron) *is entitled* to certain assets (equipment) of the company.

Ron felt much better.

SELLING EXPENSES

A subdivision of operating expenses that records expenses incurred in the marketing and sales efforts of a company.

Example: Advertising expense

Travel expense

SERIAL BONDS

All the bonds of a certain issue of a company do not come due (or mature) at once.

Parts of the bond issue mature or come due for payment at different times.

Serial Bonds

James Stores, Inc., who had raised money for plant expansion by selling serial bonds (January 1999), issued the following dates when portions of its $100,000 bond issue will be paid back:

		Serial Numbers
January 2005	$ 25,000	1-250
January 2010	25,000	251-500
January 2015	25,000	501-750
January 2020	25,000	751-1000
	$100,000	

By January 2020, all bonds will be paid back (here interest has not been discussed).

SINKING FUND BONDS

Bonds that require that a special reserve or fund be set up (to accumulate money) that will make sure the company will be able to pay off the bonds when they become due (reach maturity).

Sinking Fund Bonds

Jangles Inc., in need of paying off current debts, issued $100,000 worth of sinking fund bonds at 6% for 10 years to investors.

The stipulation with the bonds was that each year Jangles Inc. must set up a sinking fund to accumulate the money (approximately $10,000 per year) in order to make sure the company will be able to meet its obligations when the bonds come due.

Jangles Inc. could invest money from the sinking fund in *relatively stable* income- (money-) producing securities.

SIX PERCENT, 60-DAY METHOD

A shortcut method of calculating interest (or the cost of using someone else's money) instead of the traditional formula of:

P	×	R	×	T	=	Interest
(Principal)		(Rate of Interest)		(Time)		(Interest)

The 6%, 60-day method will only be a shortcut if the math doesn't get too complicated.

Six Percent, 60-Day Method

What is the interest on $1,200 at 6% for 20 days?

6% 60 Day Method	Traditional Method
1. 6% (per year) for 60 days (1/6 of a year) is equal to 1%	$I = \$1,200 \times .06 \times {}^{20}\!/_{360}$
2. 6% for 60 days on $1,200 = $12.00 (1% x $1,200 = $12.00)	$I = \$1,200 \times .06 \times {}^{1}\!/_{18}$
3. 6% for 20 days on $1,200 = $\frac{1}{3}$(12) or $4.00	$I = 72 \times {}^{1}\!/_{18} = \$4.00$
4. Review: A. 6% 60 days for $1,200 = $12.00 B. 6% 20 days $1,200 = $\frac{1}{3}$ of "A" =$4.00	$I = \$4.00$

SLIDE

An error in writing a number by adding or deleting zeroes.

Slide

$542 = $54.20

Five hundred and forty-two was written as fifty-four dollars and twenty cents by mistake.

SOLE PROPRIETORSHIP

A business owned by one person.

SOURCE DOCUMENT

A printed or written evidence of a business transaction.

Example: Paid receipts

SPECIAL JOURNALS

A book or place (journal) where groups of similar transactions (like those involving paying of cash) are recorded.

By using special journals *rather than putting all transactions into one* general journal, *speed and accuracy, as well as organization, may result.*

Special Journals

Sales journal_____ Sale of merchandise on account

Cash receipt journal _____ Receiving money from any source

Purchase journal _____ Buying anything on account

Cash payments (disburse- _____ Money being paid for any purpose
ments) journal

Check register _____ Paying bills using a voucher system

Payroll register_____ Records payroll
(if not used as a
supplementary record)

˙ Other forms would be partnerships and corporations.

STANDARD COST

The anticipated cost that should have been incurred in producing a unit of output.

STATED VALUE OF STOCK

An arbitrary value which is assigned to a corporation's stock by its board of directors. Sometimes the board of directors designates an assigned stated value to stock with no pay value.

Not all states require a par value to be placed on a corporation's stock.

(See par value for further discussion)

Stated Value of Stock

On January 8, 200X, Howard Caras Sweaters Inc. issued 5,000 shares of no-par common stock at a stated value of $5 for $15 per share.

The following entry was recorded:

Journal   Page #1

Date		Description (Accounts)	Folio (PR)	Debit	Credit
200X Jan.	8	Cash		75,000	
		Common Stock			25,000
		Paid-in capital in excess of stated value			50,000

5,000 shares X $15 per share

5,000 shares X $ 5 per share

STATEMENT ANALYSIS

Taking financial reports (or statements) and trying to hopefully interpret or better understand the operations and financial position of a company as of a specific period of time or as of a certain date.

(See comparative, vertical, or horizontal for more detail)

STOCK

Basic Ownership in a Corporation

A. To an Investor

This is a piece of paper (called a stock certificate) showing the amount or ownership and rights one has in a corporation.

Depending upon the type of stock as well as the amount purchased, different rights and ownership will develop.

B. To a Corporation

This is a means or way of raising money (capital) by selling shares of stock to investors.

Stock

Mighty Wool Inc. issued 50,000 shares of $10 par stock to investors at $20 per share.

A: *To an Investor*

One now has bought ownership and rights into Mighty Wool (depending on amount bought).

B. *To the Corporation*

Might Wool Inc. has raised $1,000,000 (50,000 shares x $20 per share) by selling some stock.

STOCK CERTIFICATE

Piece(s) of paper(s) which shows or verifies the amount of ownership and rights one (stockholder) has in a corporation.

(See preferred stock)

STOCK DIVIDEND

The amount of stock that a corporation divides or gives out to the stockholders of the corporation without receiving money from the stock given out.

There is no cash being given to the stockholders.

The corporation transfers or takes an amount from retained earnings (accumulated earnings) and places it into paid-in capital.

This means earnings are kept in the corporation instead of being paid out as in a cash dividend.

(See stock split)

Stock Dividend

Joanne Soterpolus owns 1,000 shares of Beep Corporation.

On July 10, she received notice of a 5% stock dividend issued by the company.

Joanne was thrilled, but her best friend, Kath Spaneas, told her, "Don't be too excited, the company is giving all the stockholders a 5% dividend, which means you really own the same proportion of the corporation as before."

Before	*After*
1,000 shares = $\dfrac{1}{100}$ of all stock	1,050 = $\dfrac{1}{100}$ of all stock

STOCK SPLIT

A method usually used by a corporation to reduce the market price of its common stock, which would hopefully cause more people to invest in it. The stock split is the issuance of a large number of shares to stockholders when no new assets are contributed to the firm.

The method reduces the par value of the corporation's common stock.

The corporation can then issue more common stock to the stockholders to make up for the reduction in par value.

(See stock dividend)

Stock Split

The stock of Baby Industries (50,000 shares issued at $20 par) was selling on the stock exchange for $200 per share.

The board of directors of Baby Industries declared a two-for-one stock split (with the idea of reducing the price of the stock to $100) to encourage more investors to buy the stock.

Corporation Stock Structure

Before Split	*After Split*
50,000 shares at $20 par	100,000 shares at $10 par

Before

John Mills originally owned *100 shares* of Baby Industries at a market value of *$200 per share,* or the total value of his stock was $200,000.

After

John now has *200 shares* at a market value of *$100 per share,* or his stock is worth $200,000.

Things haven't changed.

STOCKHOLDERS (SHAREHOLDERS)

The owners of a corporation.

The owners have bought or have received shares of stock that show the amount of their ownership and rights in a company. One must keep in mind that a corporation, in the eyes of the law, is separate from its owner. The corporation is an artificial person in the eyes of the law. Keep in mind that individuals and companies can be stockholders.

STOCKHOLDER'S EQUITY (CAPITAL)
(SHAREHOLDER'S EQUITY)

Claims of the owners (who have bought or received stock) of a corporation to things or assets in that corporation.

These rights of the owners vary depending on what type of stock the owner has (common stock, preferred stock, etc.).

Stockholder's Equity	=	Paid-in Capital	+	Retained Earnings
(For the usuals, see paid-in cap. for help)		Usually the amount of money that a corp. rec. from selling (or issuing) stock to investors		The profit that has been kept or has accumulated in the business rather than being paid out (dividends, etc.)

Stockholder's Equity (Shareholder's Equity)

Paid-in capital (contributed capital):

Common stock	$200,000	
Retained earnings	40,000	
Total stockholder's equity		$240,000

STRAIGHT-LINE METHOD OF DEPRECIATION

A method used to spread (or allocate) the total amount of depreciation related to a plant asset (equipment, building, etc.) over its estimated life.

This method spreads the depreciation expense equally over a number of years (the life estimation of the asset).

$$\frac{\text{Cost of plant asset} - \text{salvage value}}{\text{Number of years to be depreciated}} = \text{depreciation expense taken each year}$$

(See declining-balance, sum-of-years, and units of production)

Straight-Line Method of Depreciation

Facts:

1. Tremblay Corporation bought a truck for $5,000.

2. Residual (scrap, trade-in, etc.) value is $500.

3. Estimated life, 9 years.

$$\text{Annual depreciation} = \frac{\$5,000 - \$500}{9 \text{ years}} = \$500 \text{ per year}$$

	Depreciation	Accumulated Depreciation at End of Each Year	Book Value
Year 1	$500	$ 500	$4,500
2	500	1,000	4,000
3	500	1,500	3,500
4	500	2,000	3,000
5	500	2,500	2,500
6	500	3,000	2,000
7	500	3,500	1,500
8	500	4,000	1,000
9	500	4,500	500

SUBSCRIPTIONS (RECEIVABLE)

One way or method a corporation uses to sell its stock (especially when a corporation has just been organized).

1. *Under this method, the investor subscribes or "signs up" for a certain amount of stock.*

    The investor promises to pay the corporation for the stock in the future (one payment or installment).

    The corporation then has an asset called common stock subscriptions receivable.

2. After *the corporation receives full payment from the investor, the corporation issues the stock certificate(s).*

Subscriptions (Receivable)

John Dunn Corporation received subscriptions for 5,000 shares of $5 par common stock from investors (subscribers) at $6 per share, with a down payment of 50% of the subscription price.

						Explanation
March	1	Com. Stock Sub. Rec.	30,000			5,000 Shrs. @ $6/Shr. = $30,000
		Common Stock Sub.		25,000		5,000 Shrs @ $5/Shr. = $25,000
		Premium on Com. Stk.		5,000		30,000 — 25,000 = 5,000 Pre.
(Down	1	Cash	15,000			2,500 Shrs. x $6/Per Shr.
Payment)		Common Stk. Sub. Rec.		15,000		= $15,000

Received 25% of subscription price from all subscribers.

May	1	Cash	7,500			1,250 Shrs. x $6/Per Share
		Common Stk. Sub. Rec.		7,500		= $7,500

Received final 25% of subscription price from all subscribers and issued the stock certificates.

July	1	Cash	7,500			1,250 Shrs. x $6/Per Share
		Common Stk. Sub. Rec.		7,500		= $7,500
	1	Common Stock Subscribed	25,000			5,000 Shrs. x $5/Per Share
		Common Stock		25,000		= $25,000

SUBSIDIARY COMPANY

A business owned and controlled by another company (called the parent company).

Jones Electric owns 80% of the stock of Mayberry Light.

SUM-OF-THE-YEARS-DIGIT METHOD OF DEPRECIATION

A method used to spread (or allocate) the total amount of depreciation related to a plant asset (equipment, building, etc.) over its estimated life.

This method is similar to the declining-balance method in that it takes more or accelerates depreciation in the early years of the plant asset, *but this method does its calculations on a fractional basis (sum of number of years to be depreciated = denominator, and years left to be depreciated is the numerator) versus the declining-balance, which uses a percentage rate.*

This method uses *salvage value (residual value).*

(See declining-balance method)

Sum-of-the-Years-Digit Method of Depreciation

Facts: Cost of truck $31,000
        Residual value   1,000
        Estimated life   5 years

Year	Cost, Less Residual X Rate*	Depreciation Expense for Year	Accumulated Depreciation End of Year	Book Value End of Year (Cost-accu. dep.)
1	30,000 X 5/15	$10,000	$10,000	$21,000 (31,000 – 10,000)
2	30,000 X 4/15	8,000	$18,000 (10,000 + 8,000)	$13,000 (31,000 – 18,000)
3	30,000 X 3/15	6,000	$24,000 (18,000 + 6,000)	$7,000 (31,000 – 24,000)
4	30,000 X 2/15	4,000	$28,000 (24,000 + 4,000)	$3,000 (31,000 – 28,000)
5	30,000 X 1/15	2,000	$30,000 (28,000 + 2,000)	$1,000 (31,000 – 30,000)

$$*5 + 4 + 3 + 2 + 1 = 15 \text{ or } s = \frac{N(N+1)}{2} = \frac{5(5+1)}{2} = \frac{5(6)}{2} = 15$$

SUNDRY ACCOUNT COLUMN (MISCELLANEOUS ACCOUNT)
*A column in a journal which records parts of miscellaneous transactions (or transactions that do not occur too often).**

Cash Receipts Journal			Page 1
Accounts Credited	PR	Sundry Cr.	
R. Jones Capital	310	120,000	
Notes Payable	212	110,000	
Totals		130,000	
		(X)	

* If transactions occur too often, a special column would be set up, so as not to abuse the sundry column.

SUNK COST

Cost incurred in the past which cannot be changed by current decision(s) facing the firm.

T-ACCOUNT

A simplified device or place for demonstration that looks like the letter "T" which records and summarizes individual accounts (asset, liability, capital [owner's equity], revenue, expenses, drawing); also, income summary (expenses and revenue summary).

(See account)

T-Account

Cash		Account No. 1	
Jan. 1 Bal. 10		Nov. 1	5
Jan. 10	15		

TERM BONDS

All bonds of a certain issue come due (or mature) at once.

Term Bonds

Jon Lynch Inc. had raised money for plant expansion, as well as for paying off current debts, by selling term bonds ($100,000 worth, at 6% per year payable on January 1, 199X).

On January 1, 200X, Jon Lynch Inc. paid back the $100,000. (Or we say the bonds issued had come due *all at once*).

TRADE DISCOUNTS

Reductions from the list or retail price offered by many manufacturers and wholesalers.

A trade discount has no relation to cash discount, which deals with prompt payment.

Trade Discount

Gem Wholesalers offered rings for $2,000 (with a trade discount of 10%) to its customers.

$2,000   x   10%   = $200 Trade Discount

$2,000   – $200   = $1,800

Selling price of ring
before discount
$2,000

Trade Discount
$200

Selling price of ring
after discount
$1,800

Key Point: Trade discounts are not recorded.

TRADE-IN VALUE

A portion of the cost of a plant asset (equipment) that one can get back when it is removed or has reached the end of its productive life.

Trade-in value is hard to estimate but gives us an estimate of how much depreciation should be taken on a plant asset (equipment) over its lifetime.

Equipment – trade-in value = amount of depreciation to be taken over the lifetime of the plant asset.

Trade-In Value

Warren Ford bought a new truck for his sales fleet for $25,000.

Based on guidelines set up by the Internal Revenue Service, as well as past history of his other vehicles, Warren estimated in five years he could sell or trade the truck in the marketplace for $3000.

Warren calculated he would depreciate the truck $22,000 over the next 5 years.

Truck	–	trade-in value	=	amount to be depreciated
$25,000	–	$3000	=	$22,000

TRANSACTIONS

Exchanges of goods and services that are recorded in the journals of a business.

Transactions

Buy a building
Pay phone bill
Make a sale in a store
Buy equipment

Buy some supplies
Invest money in a business
Withdraw money out of a business

TRANSPOSITION

Rearranging digits by mistake.

Transposition

Writing five hundred and forty-two as four hundred and fifty-two by mistake.

$$542 = 452$$

TREASURY STOCK

The corporation's own stock that has been bought back (by the corporation) or has been given back to the corporation as a gift.

This stock had previously been issued (or sold) to investors who had fully paid for it.

This stock hasn't been cancelled nor has it been reissued again.

Treasury stock is not an asset. It loses many of the rights of common stock.

Treasury Stock

On February 1, 2000, Maybell Corporation bought back 2,000 shares of its stock from investors for $50 per share. The following was recorded:

Journal   Page #1

Date			Description (Accounts)	Folio (PR)	Debit	Credit
200X Feb.	1		Treasury stock		100,000	
			Cash			100,000

Treasury stock reduces stockholder's equity. It would be shown on the balance sheet as follows:

Stockholder's Equity

Paid-in capital	$100,000
Common stock 10 par, 100,000 shares	
Retained earnings	50,000
Total	$150,000
Deduct treasury stock (2,000	– 100,000
shares @ $50 per share)	
Total stockholder's equity	$ 50,000

TRIAL BALANCE

A list of the ledger (group of accounts) to test equality of debits and credits.

(See post-closing trial balance)

Trial Balance

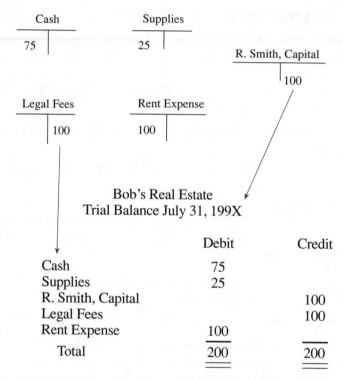

Cash		Supplies	
75		25	

R. Smith, Capital

| | 100 |

Legal Fees		Rent Expense	
	100	100	

Bob's Real Estate
Trial Balance July 31, 199X

	Debit	Credit
Cash	75	
Supplies	25	
R. Smith, Capital		100
Legal Fees		100
Rent Expense	100	
Total	200	200

(The trial balance is listed in the following order: assets, liabilities, capital, withdrawals, revenue, and expenses.)

UNADJUSTED TRIAL BALANCE

The trial balance (list of the ledger) before it is updated by adjusting entries.

(See adjusted trial balance, adjusting entries)

Unadjusted Trial Balances

December 31, 200X

	Debit	Credit
Cash	100	
Accounts Receivable	200	
Supplies	300	
Equipme nt	400	
Accumulated depreciation—equipment		100
J. Smith, capital		100
J. Smith, withdrawal	200	
Legal fees		1,000
Total	1,200	1,200

Actually, supplies should be $200 ($100 of supplies had been used up during the year), and accumulated depreciation should be $200 ($100 of depreciation taken each year on equipment). These will be updated by adjusting entries which will then form the following trial balance:

Adjusted Trial Balance

	Debit	Credit
Cash	100	
Accounts Receivable	200	
Supplies	300	
Equipment	400	
Accumulated depreciation—equipment		200
J. Smith, capital		100
J. Smith, withdrawal	200	
Legal fees		1,000
Supplies expense	100	
Depreciation expense	100	
Total	1,300	1,300

UNDERAPPLIED OVERHEAD

The situation where less overhead was transferred to work in process than estimated or incurred. The balance of the account is a debit.

UNDERWRITER

Dealers or brokers in investment companies that buy stocks or bonds (type of securities) from a corporation with the intent to resell *these securities to the public.*

Underwriter

James Securities, an underwriter, bought a new issue of stock from Mick's Department Store. James Securities will *resell* this stock to investors at a higher price.

The result is that Mick's Department Store didn't have to worry about selling their stock to many different investors, while James Securities makes a profit from reselling the stock to investors.

UNEARNED REVENUE

A liability which results when a company receives money in advance revenue before the company delivers the goods or service. The company postpones recognizing the revenue until they earn it (sometimes called advances by customers).

Unearned Revenue

January 1: *Spice* magazine received $100 from Pam Sisto for payment of a one-year subscription to *Spice*.

Since *Spice* magazine hadn't really earned *any* of the sale (until they start sending the magazine), the following entry was recorded by *Spice*:

Journal   Page #1

Date		Description (Accounts)	Folio (PR)	Debit	Credit
200X Dec.	31	Cash	1	100	
		Unearned revenue	10		100

Unearned revenue is a liability — *Spice Magazine owes* a service to Pam Sisto (a *liability* called unearned revenue). Unearned revenue is a liability and not a sale.

When *Spice* earns the sale, or part of the sale, they will reduce their *liability* (by a debit to unearned revenue) and will show a sale (a credit to earned revenue).

Remember, unearned revenue is a liability.

Spice postpones the recognition of a sale until they *earn* it.

UNITS-OF-PRODUCTION (OUTPUT) METHOD OF DEPRECIATION

A method used to spread (or allocate) the total amount of depreciation related to a plant asset (equipment) over its estimated production life.

This method estimates the depreciation based on the units of production by a machine (plant asset). The formula used is:

$$\frac{\text{Cost of plant} \quad - \quad \text{Salvage}}{\begin{array}{l}\text{Total estimate of the units of} \\ \text{production for the lifetime of} \\ \text{the plant asset} \\ \text{(life hours of machine)}\end{array}} = \begin{array}{l}\text{Depreciation taken per} \\ \text{unit of production (or} \\ \text{hours machine has run)}\end{array}$$

Units-of-Production Method of Depreciation

Facts: Machine cost   = $10,000
        Salvage   = $ 1,000
        Life hours of machine =   9,000 hours

$$\frac{\$10,000 - \$1,000}{9,000} = \$1.00 \text{ an hour}$$

If machine runs for 200 hours the first year, $200 ($1.00/per hour X 200 hours) of depreciation will result.

UNLIMITED LIABILITY

If a business (not corporation) falls into debt, the owner(s) of that business may be *liable* for paying or settling the debts of the business from personal assets (savings accounts, home, car).

(For comparison, see limited liability)

Unlimited Liability

Jim's Sporting Goods (a sole proprietorship) opened for business on January 1, 1991.

On June 1, 2001, Jim's Sporting Goods faced heavy losses and was forced to go out of business.

Jim had so many bills to pay (the creditors) that he was forced to sell *his home* in order to pay off the *debts* of the business.

VARIABLE COST

Cost which varies directly as the level of the firm's operations increases or decreases.

VARIABLE COSTING

The procedure in product-costing in which only variable manufacturing costs are identified with a product, i.e. direct labor and materials and variable manufacturing overhead. Usually this is an internal management tool. The fixed costs are treated as end-of-period costs.

(See absorption costing)

VARIANCE

Difference (favorable or unfavorable) that arises between standard and actual costs.

VERTICAL ANALYSIS OF STATEMENTS

One way of understanding or interpreting comparative statements.

This way will hopefully give a better understanding of the operations and financial position of a company as of a specific period of time, or as of a certain date.

This method relates or groups each figure to a base figure (going down the columns).

(See example)

(See horizontal analysis, comparative statements)

Vertical Analysis of Statements

	2002		2001		
	Am't	Perc. *	Am't	Perc. **	
Assets					
Current assets	25	25%	10	20%	
Long-term investments	20	20%	20	40%	
Plant assets	20	20%	10	20%	*25 =25%
Intangible assets	35	35%	10	20%	100
Total assets	100	100%	50	100%	(base figure)
Liabilities				***	
Current liabilities	10	10%	5	10%	** 10 =20%
Long-term liabilities	20	20%	20	40%	50
Total liabilities	30	30%	25	50%	(base figure)
Stockholder's equity					
Common stock	50	50%	20	40%	*** 5 =10%
Retained earnings	20	20%	5	10%	50
Total stockholder's equity	70	70%	25	50%	(base figure)
Total liabilities and stockholder's equity	100	100%	50	100%	

VOUCHER

A form or piece of paper used in an internal control system which is used to contain and verify all information about a bill (or obligation) to be processed or paid.

Usually the original bill is then attached to the voucher. The voucher and bill are filed together in an unpaid voucher file until time of payment is due.

(See voucher register, check register)

Voucher

	Voucher		
	Art Calnan Auto Supplies, Inc.		
Date	July 1, 2001	Voucher Number	430
Payee	Cassidy Company		
	3 Essex Street		
	Beverly, MA 01915		

Date	Details	Amount
July 1, 2001	Invoice No. 2333	$300.00
	FOB Beverly 2/10, n/30	
	Attach supporting documents	

VOUCHERS PAYABLE

When a company uses a voucher system, vouchers payable takes the place of the account called accounts payable.

Vouchers payable means we owe some money.

When the company pays what it owes, it reduces vouchers payable and decreases its cash.

Vouchers Payable (Accounts Payable)

John Mizex Corporation (which uses a voucher system) bought $500 of merchandise on account from Kyleen Co.

The following was entered into the voucher register:

(1) A debit to purchases
(2) A credit to vouchers payable (that we owe money)

Purchases	Vouchers Payable
500	500

222

VOUCHER REGISTER

When a company uses a voucher system, the voucher register *takes the place of the* purchase journal.

Any expense or purchase that will require payment (cash or check) will be recorded into the voucher (an expanded type of purchase journal) register. A paid voucher file is used to contain the paid vouchers in numerical sequence.

(See check register)

Voucher Register

Date	Voucher Number	Payee (One who will receive	Payment Date	Check	Voucher Payable Credit	Purchs. (Debits)	Freight (Debits) Debit	Miscellaneous Accounts Debit Ac. Name	Am't
Feb.									
10	3	Kesler Inc.	3/10	911	$300	$300			
12	5	Russell	3/12	912	350	300	50		
15	8	Supplies.com	3/15	913	200			Off. Sup.	$200

1. We bought merchandise from Kesler Inc. for resale for $300 on Feb. 10. We paid off (or reduced voucher payable by $300) by writing a check from our check register on March 10.

2. We bought merchandise from Russell Sales for $300 (plus $50 for freight) on Feb. 12. We paid off (or reduced vouchers payable by $350) by writing a check from our check register on March 12.

3. We bought supplies (not for resale) from Supplies.com on Feb. 15. We paid off (or reduced vouchers payable by $200) by writing a check.

(See check register for comparison)

VOUCHER SYSTEM

A type of internal control system (usually for a large company) which controls the cash (checks) being spent (or written).

This system tells the person paying the bills (obligations) that these obligations are true and proper and should be paid.

(See internal control)

Voucher System

Made up of:
Vouchers
Voucher file (paid and unpaid)
Voucher register (takes place of purchase journal)
Check register (takes place of cash disbursements journal)
General journal
(See individual item for detail)

W-2

a Control number 22222	Void ☐	For Official Use Only ▶ OMB No. 1545-0008		
b Employer's identification number 58-12134791		**1** Wages, tips, other compensation 71,500.00		**2** Federal income tax withheld 11,544.00
c Employer's name, address, and ZIP code Joe's Market 10 Lovett Road Salem, MA 01920		**3** Social security wages 60,600.00		**4** Social security tax withheld 3,757.20
		5 Medicare wages and tips 71,500.00		**6** Medicare tax withheld 1,036.75
		7 Social security tips		**8** Allocated tips
d Employee's social security number 021-36-9494		**9** Advance EIC payment		**10** Dependent care benefits
e Employee's name (first, middle initial, last) Joyce Royal 80 Garfield Street Marblehead, MA 01945		**11** Nonqualified plans		**12** Benefits included in box 1
		13 See Instrs. for box 13		**14** Other

	15 Statutory employee ☐	Deceased ☐	Pension plan ☐	Legal rep. ☐	942 emp. ☐	Subtotal ☐	Deferred compensation ☐
f Employee's address and ZIP code							

16 State	Employer's state I.D. No.	17 State wages, tips, etc.	18 State income tax	19 Locality name	20 Local wages, tips, etc.	21 Local income tax
MA	6 21-8966-4	71,500	3,575.00			

Cat. No. 10134D   Department of the Treasury—Internal Revenue Service

Form **W-2** Wage and Tax Statement **199X**

For Paperwork Reduction Act Notice, see separate instructions.

Copy A For Social Security Administration

W-2

A statement sent or given to an employee (worker) of a business which shows the gross earnings and deductions (FICA, federal income tax) for a calendar year which is used for income tax purposes.

The business sends a copy of the W-2 to the state, as well as to the Internal Revenue Service.

The worker attaches a copy of the W-2 to his Federal and State Income Tax Returns.

(See calendar year, W-4)

W-4

A form (filled out by a new employee, or an old employee who wants to change the figures in the form) which provides the proper information to the business to calculate a worker's state and federal income taxes to be withheld.

(See W-2)

Form **W-4** Department of the Treasury Internal Revenue Service	**Employee's Withholding Allowance Certificate** ► For Privacy Act and Paperwork Reduction Act Notice, see reverse.		OMB No. 1545-0010 **199X**
1 Type or print your first name and middle initial JOYCE	Last name ROYAL		2 Your social security number 021 ⋮ 36 ⋮ 9494
Home address (number and street or rural route) 80 GARFIELD STREET	3 ☐ Single ☐ Married ☒ Married, but withhold at higher Single rate. Note: If married, but legally separated, or spouse is a nonresident alien, check the Single box.		
City or town, state, and ZIP code MARBLEHEAD, MA 01945	4 If your last name differs from that on your social security card, check here and call 1-800-772-1213 for more information · · · · ► ☐		
5 Total number of allowances you are claiming (from line G above or from the worksheets on page 2 if they apply) .		**5**	3
6 Additional amount, if any, you want withheld from each paycheck		**6** $	
7 I claim exemption from withholding for 1994 and I certify that I meet **BOTH** of the following conditions for exemption: • Last year I had a right to a refund of **ALL** Federal income tax withheld because I had **NO** tax liability; **AND** • This year I expect a refund of **ALL** Federal income tax withheld because I expect to have **NO** tax liability. If you meet both conditions, enter "EXEMPT" here . . . . ►		**7**	

Under penalties of perjury, I certify that I am entitled to the number of withholding allowances claimed on this certificate or entitled to claim exempt status.

Employee's signature ► *Joyce Royal*	Date ► January 2 , 19 9X	
8 Employer's name and address (Employer: Complete 8 and 10 only if sending to the IRS)	9 Office code (optional)	10 Employer identification number

Cat. No. 10220Q

Key Point: The W-4 doesn't provide information for deductions for FICA, savings, bonds, hospitalization, union dues, etc.

WEIGHTED AVERAGE METHOD OF INVENTORY COSTING

A method used to assign a cost or place or dollar figure to the goods remaining (ending inventory) in a business at the end of a period of time and to find the cost of the goods a business sold *during that same period of time.*

This method gets a weighted cost per unit *of all inventory (beginning inventory plus all purchases).*

(See LIFO, FIFO)

Weighted Average of Inventory Costing

J.J. Supermarket

Facts:	No. of Cans of Soup Bought for Resale	Cost Per Can	Total Cost
On Jan. 1, 200X	20	$3.00	$ 60.00
March 1	15	2.00	30.00
Nov. 3	10	1.00	10.00
Nov. 10	55	2.00	110.00
	100		$ 210.00

Weighted average cost per unit $= \dfrac{\text{total cost}}{\text{total no. of cans of soup bought}}$

$= \dfrac{210}{100}$

= $2.10 is to average cost of bringing all the soup into the store (per can of soup)

If at the end of the year 5 cans of soup are left in the store, the cost of these cans is calculated as follows:

$2.10 X 5 cans = $10.50 cost of ending inventory

WITHDRAWAL

Cash or other assets an owner takes out of his business for his own personal *satisfaction (living expense). It is not a business expense (such as salaries) but a* personal *expense. Withdrawals have a debit balance and are* not *found on the income statement.*

In a corporation, withdrawals are sometimes *called dividends.*

Withdrawals: Temporary account on the balance sheet. Normal balance is a debit.

WORK IN PROCESS ACCOUNT — MANUFACTURING COMPANY (GOODS IN PROCESS)

One type of inventory account in a manufacturing business that contains information about goods that are now in the process of being manufactured or about the work in process.*

(See also direct labor or factory overhead)

I SUPPOSE YOU COULD SAY HAVING A BABY AND BUILDING A COMPANY IS KIND OF SIMILAR! IT'S A WORK IN PROGRESS!

* The other two types of inventory:
1. Raw materials
2. Finished goods.

WORKING CAPITAL

Current assets minus current liabilities.

(See fund statement)

Working Capital

Current assets:	
Cash	$1,000
Accounts receivable	500
Inventory	300
Prepaid rent	500
Total current assets	$2,300
Current liabilities:	
Accounts payable	$ 400
Notes payable	800
Total current liabilities	$1,200

```
    Total current assets
  - Total current liabilities
  ─────────────────────────────
  = Working capital
```

WORK SHEET

A columnar form or paper which, in an orderly process, acts as a tool in gathering and summarizing accounting data on a sheet of paper that is needed in completing the accounting cycle (preparing a trial balance, adjusting entries, clearing or closing entries, preparing financial statements — balance sheet and income statement).

A work sheet can be compared to a rough draft that one uses in writing a term paper. When the completed project (like a balance sheet) is turned in, no one sees the "scrap paper" (which made the final outcome possible — like a work sheet).

Jeff Slater
December 31, 19XX

Account Titles	Trial Balance Debit	Trial Balance Credit	Adjustments Debit	Adjustments Credit	Adj. Trial Balance Debit	Adj. Trial Balance Credit	Income Statement Debit	Income Statement Credit	Balance Sheet Debit	Balance Sheet Credit
Cash	3000|00				3000|00				3000|00	
Accounts receivable	1500|00				1500|00				1500|00	
Merchandise inventory*	7000|00				7000|00		7000|00	1000|00	1000|00	
Prepaid rent	500|00			(a) 150|00	350|00				350|00	
Office supplies	600|00			(b) 230|00	370|00				370|00	
Store supplies	350|00				350|00				350|00	
Prepaid advertising	150|00			(c) 33|00	117|00				117|00	
Office furniture	10000|00				10000|00				10000|00	
Office equipment	4800|00				4800|00				4800|00	
Accumulated depreciation—off. equ.		200|00		(d) 600|00		800|00				800|00
Salaries payable		240|00		(e) 1000|00		1240|00				1240|00
Accounts payable		6650|00	(f) 700|00			5950|00				5950|00
Jeff Slater, capital		10000|00				10000|00				10000|00
Sales		27710|00				27710|00		27710|00		
Sales returns and allowances	700|00				700|00		700|00			
Sales discounts	150|00				150|00		150|00			
Purchases	12000|00				12000|00		12000|00			
Purchases discount		600|00				600|00		600|00		
Freight-in	450|00				450|00		450|00			
Salaries expense	4200|00		(e) 1000|00		5200|00		5200|00			
Rent expense			(a) 150|00		150|00		150|00			
Office supplies expense			(b) 230|00		230|00		230|00			
Advertising expense			(c) 33|00		33|00		33|00			
Depreciation expense—off. equip.			(d) 600|00		600|00		600|00			
Purchases returns and allowances				(f) 700|00		700|00		700|00		
	45400|00	45400|00	2713|00	2713|00	47000|00	47000|00	26513|00	30010|00	21487|00	17990|00
Net income (net profit)							3497|00			3497|00
							30010|00	30010|00	21487|00	21487|00

*The $7,000 of beginning merchandise inventory is assumed to be a cost and thus is placed on the debit column of the income statement on the worksheet and the ending figure for merchandise inventory ($1,000) is assumed not to be sold and thus not a cost. This ending inventory figure is the beginning inventory on the debit column of the balance sheet.

Work Sheet

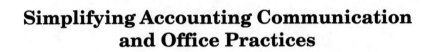

Simplifying Accounting Communication and Office Practices

Tips on Writing Memos

Every memo has two parts:
- The **identification block** has four lines:
  - To — the name(s) of the recipient(s)
  - From — the name of the sender
  - Re — the subject of the memo
  - Date — the date the memo is sent out
- The **message** consists of one or more short paragraphs on one topic.

In addition, a memo may have:
- A **banner**, which appears either above or below the identification block; for example: Confidential, Urgent, Update, Reply requested.
- An **attachment notation** — "Attached: May sales summary (2 pages)" — which appears several lines below the message, listing any documents that accompany the memo.
- A **copies notation** — "cc: Carmen Smith" — also below the message, showing who will receive a copy of the memo. ("cc" is short for "carbon copy" or "courtesy copy.")
- A **page number** — "page 1 of 2 pages" — placed below all the other items — if the memo runs more than one page.

Before you start to write a memo, ask yourself the following questions:
- What is my key purpose? For example: to inform, persuade, request, or suggest.
- Is a memo the best way to accomplish *this* purpose? Or would a phone call or face-to-face conversation be more effective?
- What is the most important thing I want the recipient to know?
- What facts do I need to convey?
- Is there a specific action I want the recipient to take?

When you start to write, put the most important information first. For example, you can use the first sentence to:
- Explain why you're writing. "Here is the list of new codes for accounts payable."
- Provide a crucial piece of background information: "As you know, this year's budget requires our department to reduce overtime by 10 percent."
- Pose a problem: "Last month, delinquent accounts increased from 53 to 75."
- State a solution: "Our new software allows us to create monthly reports without re-inputting the data."
- Offer good news: "Our company won the Groverfield account."

As you write, try not to ramble. Get to the point, and stop when you're done.

If you need a response from the recipient, put your request in a separate paragraph — and state the deadline and format for the response:
- Please put your request in my in-basket before noon on Monday, March 10.
- Call me as soon as possible (at 555-1234) if you are unable to attend the meeting.
- Please send me an e-mail (jim@acme.org) with a "yes" or "no". I need your response by 3 p.m. on Tuesday.

Be careful about saying "I'll assume this is OK if I don't hear from you." Although this offer seems to save the recipient the chore of responding, you will have no way of knowing whether the recipient has intentionally chosen not to respond or was simply unable to respond in a timely manner.

When you've finished writing your memo, reread it to make sure your message:
- restricts itself to one topic.
- Includes all the relevant facts.
- Is courteous and tactful.
- Contains short sentences and paragraphs.
- Uses typographical emphasis (bold, italics and exclamation points) sparingly, if at all.

Once you are satisfied with the content of the memo, run the spellchecker. Then carefully reread what you've written. Pay special attention to any numbers in the text and to errors that your spellchecker cannot catch. For example:

Incorrect: Form 1999 too 2022 net sails fell. We are not taking stops to reverse this trend.

Should read: From 1999 to 2002 net sales fell. We are now taking steps to reverse this trend.

(Did you catch all six mistakes in the incorrect version?)

Finally, adjust the margins so that your text is surrounded by ample white space: at least two inches at the top and about 1.5 inches at the right and left. Double-space the identification block and leave three blank lines after it. Single-space the message and add one blank line after each paragraph. If you have an attachment or cc notation, start it three lines after the end of the message.

Sensitive memos should be placed in envelopes marked "Confidential." Other memos can be distributed without envelopes as long as any attachments are securely fastened to the memo.

Tips on Writing Business Letters

Memos and e-mail are fine for informal communications, especially among people who work for the same company. But in most other situations, a full-dress letter is called for. And so, you may find yourself writing a letter:

- to apply for employment
- to introduce your services to prospective clients
- to communicate with banks
- to explain a change in procedures to current clients
- to announce new services to clients
- to respond to a client's complaint
- to request payment of an overdue bill
- to thank someone for something they have done on your behalf

The first step, simple as it may sound, is to determine the full name and address of the person you want to contact. A misdirected letter might never reach the right person, or might not reach that person in a timely manner. Also, take care to spell the recipient's name correctly. The recipient will appreciate this courtesy, and your attention to detail will add to your credibility.

Next, take a few moments to collect your thoughts:

- What is the main purpose of your letter?
- What facts will your reader need in order to understand the meaning or significance of your message?
- What documents, if any, should be enclosed?
- What actions, if any, do you want your reader to take in response to your message? What type of appeal will best motivate the reader to take the desired actions.
- What actions, if any, will you be taking?

Use the first sentence or two of your letter to explain your reason for writing. Without overstating your case, try to catch the reader's attention and concern. Then, move on to supply the relevant facts and background information. If the matter is a simple one, you may need only one or two paragraphs to convey these facts. For a complex matter, you may need a page or more. The goal is to include all the information the reader needs without confusing the issue by raising irrelevant details.

In the closing paragraph, look toward the future: Tell the reader what actions you will take, or ask the reader to take a specific step. For example:

- I will phone you as son as I have tracked down the information you requested.
- I will send you the report as soon as it is completed.
- Please call me to arrange an interview.
- Please let me know if this change is acceptable.
- If you need more information, please call me.

After you have finished your first draft, put it aside for at least a few minutes, if not overnight. When you return to it, pretend that the letter is addressed to you and notice how it makes you feel. If the letter sounds courteous and sincere, then you're ready to move on to the next step. But is the letter sounds angry, shrill, sarcastic or dismissive, you need to fix the tone before doing anything else.

Now that the tone is right, read your draft again to see if you can improve the content or the style: Is the organization clear? Are the facts complete? Are the sentences concise? Are the arguments persuasive? If you are writing in response to a letter you have received, double-check to make sure you have addressed each issue raised in the original letter.

Once you are satisfied with the body of your letter, you can add the opening and closing sections. The opening section of a business letter has four parts:
- Writer's address and phone number (three lines). This block is omitted, however, if the letter is written on letterhead that shows the address and phone number.
- Date.
- Recipient's name and address (three or four lines).
- Salutation. The traditional salutation is "Dear" followed by the recipient's name and a comma. If the letter is addressed to a company or a department, rather than to an individual, the salutation line may be omitted. "Dear Sir or Madam" is now considered obsolete, as is "To Whom It May Concern."

At the end of the letter the closing block contains three items:
- A brief sign-off, usually "Sincerely" or "Yours truly," followed by a comma.
- The writer's handwritten signature.
- The writer's name (typed).

Enclosure and cc notations are placed several lines below the closing block.

There are many acceptable formats for laying out a business letter on the page; the most common are illustrated in the sample letters.

After you have formatted your letter, run the spellchecker — but remember not to rely on it — and correct any mistakes. Print out the letter and read it one last time — a careful word-by-word reading to make sure that everything is, as they say, letter-perfect.

A word about form letters: There are occasions when it is efficient and effective to compose one letter and send it to many individuals, changing only the recipient's address and the salutation. One appropriate use would be writing to clients to advise them of a change in your procedures, by composing one letter and use the computer's mail-merge feature to generate a "personal" copy addressed to everyone on your mailing list.

In certain situations, you should treat each letter in a batch as a separate piece of correspondence. For example, if you are applying for jobs, personalize each letter with at least a sentence or two directed at the particular company. Even if you are sending out ten letters a week, try to make each letter sound as though you are applying to for a particular job for a particular reason. In addition, when responding to help-wanted ads, tailor your letter to match the terms used in the ad. If the ad is for a "full-charge bookkeeper," use that phrase; if the ad mentions "administrative assistant" or "marketing trainee" use those words.

Tips on Sending Faxes

There are two ways to fax documents: (1) feed pieces of paper into a fax machine, or (2) generate the document on a computer and use the computer's fax-modem to send the document (not the computer file itself, just a printout of the document) over the phone lines. Fax machines are excellent for transmitting standard-size documents that are typed on white paper. Any handwritten notations should be in black ink. If the original is on gray or colored paper, you may be able to improve the clarity of the copy the recipient receives by photocopying the original (on a copier that allows you to increase the contrast) and faxing the photocopy. If the original is in a small typeface, try setting the enlargement feature on the photocopier to 105% and fax the photocopy.

For fax-modem transmissions, the type in the document should be at least 11 points, and the margins should be at least one inch on all sides. Extremely small type may not be clear or readable on the recipient's fax output.

When you send a fax, remember that many people at a company may share one fax machine, and that the machine may be in the company's mailroom. Therefore, the first page of your fax transmission should state the full name of the intended recipient. If you are sending a fax to a large company, include the name of the recipient's department and his or her phone extension, office number or other identifier.

Because corporate fax machines are not private, you should not fax sensitive information unless the recipient can assure you that the confidentiality will be maintained. Also, many corporate fax machines are unattended; that is, there is no one sitting by the machine watching the faxes come in and assembling the pages. Therefore it is crucial that the first page of a fax indicates how many pages are being sent, and that each page is numbered. For extra protection, place your name and the name of the recipient in a header or footer on each page.

Finally, at an unattended fax machine, incoming faxes may sit in the paper tray for several hours. If time is of the essence, call and alert the recipient that the document has been faxed.

Tips on Using E-mail

When you open the Write or Compose New Message feature to write an e-mail, a formatted identification block appears; you fill in the e-mail address of the recipient and the subject. The e-mail software automatically supplies your name, your e-mail address, and the date and time.

The identification block also has lines for attachment and cc notations, even "bcc"(blind courtesy copy) notations if you do not want the recipient to know who else is receiving a copy of the message.

The basic principles of memo-writing apply to electronic messages as well: Know your purpose and stick to it. Be brief, be polite, and be clear. Do not write in a very informal style. Use standard English. Spell check your text and reread it word-by-word before you press the "Send" button. Remember not to depend upon the spell checker; it cannot catch typo's that are real words (typing "cat" instead of "car") and homonyms (words that sound alike but have different meaning, such as scent, sent, and cent).

Because most people read their e-mail on-screen, you should make every effort to keep your message short. If you must write a long note, use headings to draw the reader's attention to the significant points.

Many e-mail programs allow you to specify a priority for the message — for example, high, regular, or low priority — to distinguish your e-mail message, but use this appropriately.

Outgoing e-mail can be sent with the automatic reply or confirmation feature found in most programs, whereby when the e-mail is opened by the recipient, the sender is notified that it has been received and opened, thus presumably read.

Do not send sensitive, confidential, or insulting material, nor anything that you would not want to become public. E-mail is not private! Someone other than the intended recipient might see the message. E-mail systems using networks and servers can be tracked, archived, and read by others (i.e., managers). You may delete or "trash" an e-mail, but it may remain on a network or server computer. Many lawsuits have involved subpoenaed e-mail files that were saved or recovered.

Check your e-mail frequently and regularly. Many people have the expectation of a rapid response to their e-mail message.

Be very cautious when opening an attachment from an unknown person or firm. Some people never open these, because they may contain computer viruses!

To save time, use the filter capability of your e-mail program to automatically sort incoming e-mail into predetermined folders or files.

Tips for Preparing a Presentation

Financial and accounting data are often presented to committees, boards, and groups. Here are some tips and ideas to be more efficient in preparing a presentation and more effective in delivering it.

Use the right software. If selecting new software, choose software compatible with existing software if possible, so that you can transfer data and text material easily. Then you can prepare text, charts, or spreadsheets in familiar software.

Use the right size type and appropriate fonts. Avoid large white background areas. For projected media, such as slides, use dark backgrounds with light-colored text. You may need to change the colors for the typical lighting conditions. Generally, visibility and readability, the brighter the room light, the lighter the background color. In a room with bright lighting, a light-colored background with dark text may be preferable.

If you have handouts or documents to distribute, be sure that you confirm the number of people attending so that you have an adequate supply, and that everyone has the same documents.

Call ahead to the client or site where the presentations will be delivered, to get details about the room and equipment that will be available. Find out if the room will be illuminated or if it will be or can be dark. Some rooms may not have shades or blinds; attendees may prefer a lighted room for notetaking and discussions.

If you have specific requirements, such as a slide projector, overhead projector, electrical extension cords, chalk or white board, podium, make sure in advance that such items will be available. Bring voltage converters if presenting your material out of the United States. Specialty items such as portable projection systems can be rented, if you don't have one, or if the presentation site cannot provide one. If you need a larger monitor, a TV may be usable, but only with a special modulator/adapter and TV cable. Some notebook computers support video output; others require special adapter/converters. A wireless remote control and laser pointer will allow you to roam the room or be further from your computer and the screen.

Bring a backup copy of your software and files. Some on-line services offer web-based data storage that will allow you to back up your presentation and download it if necessary from a web-accessible location.

TIPS ON OFFICE ATTIRE

Casual attire has become more acceptable in many companies; others allow and even encourage "Casual Fridays." Some people think this is a morale booster, others say it is a conspiracy from the marketing departments of clothing manufacturers! It is not without risks for both employer and employee; conflicts about acceptable casual-ware are common and have resulted in suspensions, terminations, demands that employees leave and get appropriately dressed, and even resulted in lawsuits!
A few guidelines can help both employee and employer:

T-SHIRTS
Following the lead of court decisions in several judicial districts, many companies have banned T-shirts because of obscene, disrespectful, and stupid sayings. Some firms allow only plain, colored T-Shirts — no wording, sayings, advertisements, proclamations, promotional shirts, tie-dyes, or shirts with photographs, designs or graphics. Other businesses have banned all T-shirts, stating that all shirts must have collars.

JEANS
Even companies where casual attire is the norm 5-days-a-week have banned blue jeans. Blue jeans are usually appropriate only in industrial settings and warehouses. And even there, torn jeans and jeans with holes in the knees or other places are not only inappropriate, they may be hazardous — loose threads can get caught in equipment and machinery, and holes can snag handles and be dangerous. And unsightly!

OTHER UNACCEPTABLE ITEMS:
Shorts, swimsuits, and Spandex.
Tank tops and halter tops.
Sheer, revealing, and/or suggestive clothing.
Sandals.
Baseball caps.
Rules against sneakers, tennis shoes, and other athletic shoes are also common.

Customers, clients, and co-workers can be offended by the clothing you wear. The loss of revenue from the loss of a client or customer, or a lost sale, can be the reason for a lay-off!

Appendix I The Accounting Scrapbook

Sample of:
1. Simplified Balance Sheet and Income Statement of a Service Company.
2. Classified Balance Sheet for a Service Company.
3. Trial Balance for a Merchandising Company.
4. Classified Balance Sheet for a Corporation.
5. Classified Multi-Step Income Statement for a Merchandise Company.
6. Work Sheet for a Service Company.
7. Work Sheet for a Merchandise Corporation.
8. Statement of Cash Flows.
9. Statement of Partners' Capital.
10. Sample Stockholder's Equity Section.

SAMPLE: Simplified Balance Sheet and Income Statement of a Service Company

Bill Lee, Attorney
Balance Sheet, November 30, 200X

Assets		**Liabilities**	
Cash	$ 1,200.00	Accounts Payable	$ 200.00
Accounts receivable	400.00		
Prepaid rent	600.00	**Owner's Equity**	
Law library	3,000.00	Bill Lee, capital	5,000.00
Total assets	$5,200.00	Total Equities	$5,200.00

Bill Lee, Attorney
Income Statement for Month Ended November 30, 200X

Revenue:
  Legal fees earned......................... $2,400
Operating expenses:
  Rent expense $600
  Salaries expense 800
  Telephone expense 100
      Total operating expense $1,500
Net Income .... $ 900

SAMPLE: Classified Balance Sheet for a Service Company

Bill Lee, Attorney
Income Statement for Month Ended November 30, 200X

Assets

Current assets:
Cash.	$ 199	
Prepaid insurance	46	
Office supplies	11	
Total current assets.		$ 256

Plant and equipment:
Automobile	$ 720	
Less accumulated depreciation	10	
Total plant and equipment		$ 710
Total assets		$ 966

Liabilities

Current liabilities:
Salaries payable.		7

Owner's Equity

Joe Green, capital, November 2, 200X.	$ 970	
Deduct October net loss	11	
Joe Green, capital, November 31, 200X–.		$ 959
Total liabilities and owner's equity		$ 966

SAMPLE: Trial Balance for a Merchandising Company

Blue Company
Trial Balance, June 30, 200X

	Dr.	Cr.
Cash	$10,430	
Accounts receivable	2,880	
Merchandise inventory	32,910	
Store supplies	390	
Office supplies	270	
Store equipment	24,610	
Accumulated depreciation, store equipment ..		$4,520
Accounts payable		3,790
B. Blue, capital		55,160
B. Blue, withdrawals	800	
Sales		18,790
Sales discounts	118	
Purchases	7,310	
Purchases returns and allowances		380
Purchases discounts		128
Sales salaries expense...................	1,340	
Rent expense..........................	1,000	
Utilities expense	260	
Totals	$82,768	$82,768

SAMPLE: Classified Balance Sheet for a Corporation

Blue Company
Balance Sheet, December 31, 200X

Assets

Current assets:

Cash.	$1,024	
Accounts receivable	1,397	
Merchandise inventory	5,023	
Prepaid expenses	136	$ 7,580
Total current assets.		

Plant and equipment:

Store equipment	$5,554		
Less accumulated depreciation . . .	1,281	$4,273	
Office equipment.	$1,196		
Less accumulated depreciation . . .	284	$ 912	
Total plant and equipment			$ 5,185
Total assets			$12,765

Liabilities

Current liabilities:

Accounts payable	$ 279	
Salaries payable.	74	
Income taxes payable	65	
Total liabilities		$ 418

Stockholder's Equity

Common stock, $10 par value	$6,000	
Retained earnings	6,347	
Total stockholder's equity		$12,347
Total liabilities and stockholder's equity .		$12,765

SAMPLE: Classified Multi-Step Income Statement for a Merchandise Company

Moore Company
Income Statement for Year Ended December 31, 200X

Revenue:
Sales .... $ 530,480
Less sales returns and
allowances 4,470
Net sales .... $ 526,010

Cost of Goods Sold:
Merchandise inventory,
January 1, 200X– .... $ 49,940
Purchases .... $ 337,150
Less: purchases returns
and allow. $1,790
purchases
discounts 5,940 8,730
Net Purchases .... $ 328,420
Add freight-in 4,830
Cost of goods purchased .... $ 333,250
Goods available for sale .... $ 383,190
Merchandise inventory,
December 31, 200X– 46,360
Cost of goods sold .... $ 336,830
Gross profit on sales .... $ 189,180

Operating Expenses:
Selling expenses:
Sales salaries expense ... $ 29,100
Rent expense, selling space 18,500
Advertising expense 4,600
Store supplies expense ... 4,100
Depreciation expense,
store equipment 2,800
Total selling expenses . $ 59,100

General and administrative
expenses:

Office salaries expense	$ 16,800	
Rent expense, office space . .	1,400	
Insurance expense	720	
Office supplies expense	348	
Depreciation expense, office equipment	795	
Total general and administrative expenses . .		$ 20,063
Total operating expenses		$ 79,163
Income from operations		$ 110,017
Less income taxes expenses .		12,480
Net Income		$ 97,537

SAMPLE: Work Sheet for a Service Company with Titles Mixed Intentionally in Trial Balance

Robert Ross
Work Sheet for Period Ended Current Date

	Trial Balance Debit	Trial Balance Credit	Adjustments Debit	Adjustments Credit	Adj. Trial Bal. Debit	Adj. Trial Bal. Credit	Income State. Debit	Income State. Credit	Balance Sheet Debit	Balance Sheet Credit
Accounts payable		4				4				4
Accounts receivable	6				6				6	
Accumulated depr., store equip.		4		(a) 2		6				6
Cash	10				10				10	
Notes payable		2				2				2
Prepaid insurance	6			(b) 2	4				4	
Rent expense	4				4		4			
Revenue from repairs		36				36		36		
Jane Flo, capital		22				22				22
Jane Flo, withdrawals	4				4				4	
Store equipment	14				14				14	
Shop supplies	8			(c) 6	2				2	
Wages expense	16		(d) 4		20		20			
	68	68								
Depreciation expense, store equip.			(a) 2		2		2			
Insurance expense			(b) 2		2		2			
Shop supplies expense			(c) 6		6		6			
Wages payable				(d) 4		4				4
			14	14	74	74	34	36	40	38
Net income							2			2
							36	36	40	40

SAMPLE: Work Sheet for a Merchandise Corporation that Adjusts Inventory

Ring Company
Work Sheet for Year Ended December 31, 19——

	Trial Balance Debit	Trial Balance Credit	Adjustments Debit	Adjustments Credit	Income State. Debit	Income State. Credit	Balance Sheet Debit	Balance Sheet Credit
Cash	6						6	
Accounts receivable	4						4	
Merchandise inventory	10		(b)12	(a)10			12	
Store supplies	8			(c) 6			2	
Store equipment	18						18	
Accumulated depr., store equip.		4		(d) 2				6
Accounts payable		4						4
Salaries payable				(e) 4				4
Common stock, $1 par value		20						20
Retained earnings		12						12
Income summary			(a)10	(b)12	10	12		
Sales		62				62		
Sales returns	2				2			
Purchases	24				24			
Purchases discounts		2				2		
Freight-in	2				2			
Salaries expense	12		(e) 4		16			
Rent expense	14				14			
Advertising expense	4				4			
Depreciation expense store equip.			(d) 2		2			
Store supplies expense			(c) 6		6			
	104	104	34	34	80	76	42	46
Net loss						4	4	
					80	80	46	46

SAMPLE: Statement of Cash Flows

Rose Corporation
Statement of Cash Flows
For the Year Ended April 30, 200X

Cash Flows from Operating Activities

Net Income		$53,700
Add (or deduct) Items Not Affecting Cash Flows		
From Operations		
Decrease in Accounts Receivable	$15,000	
Decrease in Inventory	15,000	
Increase in Prepaid Expenses	(1,800)	
Decrease in Accounts Payable	(3,000)	
Decrease in Income Tax Payable	(1,800)	
Depreciation	57,900	
Interest Expense	8,400	89,700
Net Cash Flows from Operating Activities		$143,400

Cash Flows From Investing Activities

Sale of Furniture		35,100

Cash Flows from Financing Activities

Repayment of Notes payable	$(60,000)	
issue of Common Stock	25,000	
Dividends Paid	(12,900)	
Interest Paid	(8,400)	
Net Cash Flows Used by Financing Activities		(6,300)
Net Increase in Cash Flows		$172,200

Schedule of Noncash Investing and Financing Transactions

Issue of Notes Payable for Furniture	$22,000

254

SAMPLE: Statement of Partners' Capital

BILL AND FLYNN
Statement of Partners' Capital
For the Year Ended December 31, 200X

	Anders	Budd	Total
Balance January 1, 20-0X	$ 50,000	$ 90,000	$130,000
Add: Additional investments	45,000	54,000	99,000
Capital account balances, Dec. 31, 200X before drawing charges............	$ 95,000	$144,000	$229,000
Deduct: Drawings.................	4,000	22,000	36,000
Capital account balances before 200X Income distribution	$ 81,000	$122,000	$193,000
Net Income per income statement	31,000	28,200	60,000
Capital account balances, Dec. 31, 200X	$112,800	$150,000	$253,000

SAMPLE: Stockholder's Equity Section

SMOOTH CORPORATION
Partial Balance Sheet
December 31, 200X

Stockholders' Equity:
    Paid-in capital:
        Preferred stock, 8%, par value, $100; 1,000 shares authorized,
          issued, and outstanding .... $ 100,000
        Common stock, no par value, stated value of $20 per share;
          50,000 shares authorized, issued, and outstanding 1,000,000
        Paid-in capital from donation of plant site 100,000
        Paid-in capital in excess of par value-preferred 8,000

        Total paid-in capital $1,208,000
Retained earnings...................... 570,000

        Total stockholders' equity $1,778,000

Appendix II Accounting: Common Formulas and Equations

1. Assets = Liabilities + Owner's Equity (Capital)

2. Assets = Liabilities + Owner's Equity + Revenues – Expenses – Drawing

3. Liabilities = Assets – Owner's Equity

4. Owners's Equity = Assets – Liabilities

5. Income Statement

     – Expenses

     = Net Income

Revenues

6. Balance Sheet

Assets = Liabilities + Owner's Equity

7. Statement of Change in Owner's Equity

Beginning Capital + Net Income – Drawings = Ending Capital

8.
Assets		=	Liabilities		+	Owner's Equity		+	Revenues		–	Expenses		–	Drawings	
Dr.	Cr.		Dr.	Cr.		Dr.	Cr.		Dr.	Cr.		Dr.	Cr.		Dr.	Cr.
+	–		–	+		–	+		–	+		+	–		+	–

9. Trial Balance =

	Debits	Credits
	Assets	Liabilities
+	Expenses	+ Owner's Equity
+	Drawings	+ Revenue

10. Adjustments

   Beginning Supplies (– Supplies used up) = Supplies on hand.

   Prepaid Rent (– Amount expired) = Amount of Rent paid in advance remaining.

   Equipment* (– Accumulated Depreciation) = Amount of Depreciation not taken as yet on the equipment.

   * This is historical cost and will not change.

11. The Adjusted Trial
   Balance on a work
   sheet

Debits	Credits
Assets	Liabilities
+ Expenses	+ Owner's Equity
+ Drawings	+ Accumulated Depreciation

12. Income Statement
   Columns on a work sheet

Debits	Credits
Expenses	Revenues
Net Income	

13. Balance Sheet
   Column on a
   work sheet

Debits	Credit s
Assets	Liabilities
+ Drawings	+ Accumulated Depreciation
	+ Capital
	+ Net Income

14. Post Closing Trial
   Balance
   All temporary accounts
   in ledger were cleared
   to zero by closing entries

=

Debits	Credits
Assets	Liabilities
	Owner's Equity (new)

FOR A MERCHANDISE COMPANY

15. Sales Returns and Allowances

Dr.	Cr.
+	−

Sales Discount

Dr.	Cr.
+	−

Purchases

Dr.	Cr.
+	−

Purchases Returns and Allowances

Dr.	Cr.
−	+

Purchases Discount

Dr.	Cr.
−	+

Freight

Dr.	Cr.
−	+

Merchandise Inventory

Dr.	Cr.
+	−

16. Issuing a Credit Memo or
   receiving a Debit Memo

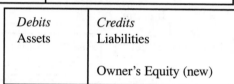

Accounts Receivable (-)
Sales Returns and Allowance (+)

17. Unearned Revenue

Dr.	Cr.
−	+

This is a liability.

258

18. Sales – Sales Returns and Allowances – Sales Discount = Net Sales
19. Net Purchases = Purchases – Purchase Discount – Purchase Ret. and Allow.
20a. Cost of goods purchased = Net Purchases + Freight
20. Merchandise (goods) Available for Sale = Beginning Inventory + Cost of Goods Purchased
21. Cost of Goods Sold = Goods available for sale – Ending Inventory
22. Gross Profit = Net Sales – Cost of Goods Sold
23. Net Income = Gross Profit – Operating Expenses

24. Bank Reconciliation

Bank	*Book*
+ Deposits in Transit	– Service Charge Collection Charge
– Checks Outstanding	– Not Sufficient Funds
+ – Bank errors	+ – Errors in recording checks, etc.
	+ - ATMs

25.

Social Security Payable		Medicare Tax Payable		State Unemployment Tax Payable	
Dr.	Cr.	Dr.	Cr.	Dr.	Cr.
–	+	–	+	–	+

Federal Unemployment		Payroll Tax Expenses	
Dr.	Cr.	Dr.	Cr.
–	+	+	–

26.

Petty Cash	
Dr.	Cr.
+	–

27.

Vouchers Payable		Discount Lost	
Dr.	Cr.	Dr.	Cr.
–	+	+	–

28. Interest = Principal x Rate x Time

29. Maturity Value = Face Value of Note + Interest on Note

30. Discount on a Note = Maturity Value x $\dfrac{\text{No. of Days Bank Holds Note}}{36}$ x Discount Rate

31. Proceeds = Maturity Value - Discount on a Note

32. 6% 60 on 500. = $5.00

33.

Bad Debt Expense			Allowance for Doubtful Accounts	
Dr.	Cr.		Dr.	Cr.
+	−		−	+

34. Accounts Receivable − Allowance for Doubtful Accounts
    = Realizable Accounts Receivable

35. Weighted Average Cost per Unit = $\dfrac{\text{\# of Units X Unit Price (Total Cost)}}{\text{Total \# of Units}}$

36. Average Cost per Unit X # of Units in Inventory = Value of
    Ending Inventory

37.

If	Overstated	Understated
Beginning Inventory	Net Income is Understated	Net Income is Overstated
Ending Inventory	Net Income is Overstated	Net Income is Understated

If Ending Inventory is Overstated, Cost of Goods sold will be Understated and thus Gross Profit as well as Net Income will be Overstated.

38. Beginning Inventory + Net Purchases + Additional Mark Ups = Merchandise Available for Sale

39. Retail Value of Goods Available for Sale − Net Sales - Mark Downs = Retail Value of Ending Inventory

40. $\dfrac{1}{\substack{\text{\# of Years to be Depreciated} \\ \text{(Useful Life)}}}$ = Annual Rate of Depreciation

41. Straight Line Depreciation = $\dfrac{\text{Cost - Salvage}}{\text{Useful Life (years)}}$

42. Units of Production = $\dfrac{\text{Cost - Salvage}}{\text{est. units of production}}$

43. Book Value = Cost − Accumulated Depreciation

44. Declining Balance
(Double)
Book Value (Beginning of Year) x Rate (Twice Straight Line)

45. Sum of Years

$$\left(\frac{\text{(reverse order of years)}}{\frac{N(N+1)}{2}} \right) \times \left(\begin{array}{c} \text{Cost} \\ -\text{ Salvage} \end{array} \right)$$

46. If Book Value = Trade-in: No gain or loss
If Book Value greater than Trade-in: Loss
If Book Value less than Trade-in: Gain

47.

Stockholder's Equity			Preferred Stock			Prem. on Stock	
Dr.	Cr.		Dr.	Cr.		Dr.	Cr.
−	+		−	+		−	+

Common Stock			Discount on Common Stock			Retained Earnings	
Dr.	Cr.		Dr.	Cr.		Dr.	Cr.
−	+		+	−		−	+

48.

Subscriptions Receivable			Common Stock Subscriptions	
Dr.	Cr.		Dr.	Cr.
+	−		−	+

Paid in Capital			Treasury Stock			Retained Earnings Appropriated	
Dr.	Cr.		Dr.	Cr.		Dr.	Cr.
−	+		+	−		−	+

49. Revenue − Cost of Goods Sold = Gross Profit − Direct Departmental expenses
= Contribution Margin − Indirect expenses = Net Income from Operations

50. Taxes due for Social Security, Medicare, and Federal Income Tax by employer.
   If an employer pays under $50,000 during the lookback period, the employer is a monthly depositor. If the employer pays $50,000 or more during this period it is considered to be a semi-weekly depositor.

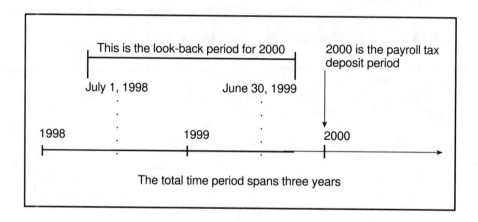

	Monday	Tuesday	Wednesday	Thursday	Friday	Saturday	Sunday
The payday occurs this week ⟶			■ If the payday occurs on one of these days, the deposit will be due Wednesday of the next week.			★ If the payday occurs on Saturday or Sunday, or...	
	★ ...Monday or Tuesday, then payroll tax deposit will be due and payable on Friday of this week.		■ Deposit day for Wednes-day–Friday payday		★ Deposit day for Saturday–Tuesday payday		

Appendix III Common Financial Ratios and Techniques

I. ASSET MANAGEMENT

1. Working Capital = Current Assets − Current Liabilities

2. Current Ratio = $\dfrac{\text{Current Assets}}{\text{Current Liabilities}}$

3. Acid Test (quick) = $\dfrac{\text{Cash \& Accounts Receivable \& Marketable Securities}}{\text{Current Liabilities}}$

4. Accounts Receivable Turnover = $\dfrac{\text{Net Sales (on account)}}{\text{Average Accounts Receivable}}$

5. Number of days' sales are tied up in accounts receivable = $\dfrac{\text{Accounts Receivable (ending)}}{\text{Average sales made on account per day}}$

6. Merchandise turnover = $\dfrac{\text{Cost of Goods (Merchandise) Sold}}{\text{Average Inventory}}$

II. DEBT CONSIDERATIONS

7. Long−term debt (Liabilities) compared to owner's equity (Capital) = $\dfrac{\text{Long−term Liabilities}}{\text{Total Equity (Capital)}}$

8. Number of times interest earned = $\dfrac{\text{Net income before interest expense \& taxes}}{\text{interest expense}}$

9. Long−term debt (Liabilities) compared to plant and equipment (fixed assets) = $\dfrac{\text{Long−term Liabilities}}{\text{Total plant \& equipment}}$

III. PERFORMANCE CONSIDERATIONS

10. Company's income to actual sales = $\dfrac{\text{Net Income}}{\text{Net Sales}}$

11. Sales Revenue produced compared to per−dollar investment in plant and equipment (fixed assets) = $\dfrac{\text{Net Sales}}{\text{Total plant \& equipment (fixed assets)}}$

12. Equity Per Share = $\dfrac{\text{Total shareholder's equity to a class of stock}}{\text{Number of shares issued and outstanding}}$

13. Rate of return on shareholder's equity for common stock

$$= \frac{\text{Net income available to common stock}}{\text{Average common stock equity}}$$

14. Rate of return on assets before taxes

$$= \frac{\text{Net income before interest expense \& taxes}}{\text{Total Assets}}$$

15. Earnings Per Share – common stock–

$$= \frac{\text{Net income—preferred stock dividends}}{\text{Average \# of outstanding shares of common stock}}$$

16. Price Earnings Ratio

$$= \frac{\text{Market Price Per Share}}{\text{Earnings Per Share}}$$

Appendix IV How to Post from Special Journals

Situation 1: Sale on Account

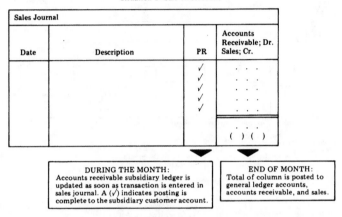

DURING THE MONTH:	END OF MONTH:
Accounts receivable subsidiary ledger is updated as soon as transaction is entered in sales journal. A (√) indicates posting is complete to the subsidiary customer account.	Total of column is posted to general ledger accounts, accounts receivable, and sales.

Situation 2: Issuing a Credit Memo without Sales Tax
Recorded in a General Journal

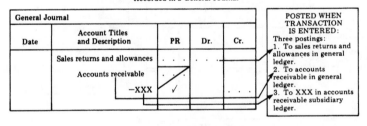

How to Post from Special Journals

Situation 4: Inflow of Cash

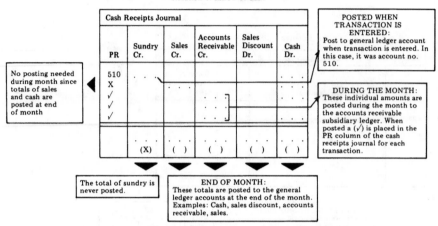

No posting needed during month since totals of sales and cash are posted at end of month

Cash Receipts Journal

PR	Sundry Cr.	Sales Cr.	Accounts Receivable Cr.	Sales Discount Dr.	Cash Dr.
510 X ✓ ✓ ✓	. . .	. . .	. .] . .]	. . .	. . . .
	. . . (X)	. . . ( )	. . . ( )	. . . ( )	. . . ( )

POSTED WHEN TRANSACTION IS ENTERED:
Post to general ledger account when transaction is entered. In this case, it was account no. 510.

DURING THE MONTH:
These individual amounts are posted during the month to the accounts receivable subsidiary ledger. When posted a (✓) is placed in the PR column of the cash receipts journal for each transaction.

The total of sundry is never posted.

END OF MONTH:
These totals are posted to the general ledger accounts at the end of the month. Examples: Cash, sales discount, accounts receivable, sales.

Situation 5: Purchase of Merchandise or Other Items on Account

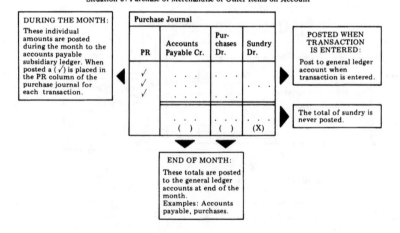

DURING THE MONTH:
These individual amounts are posted during the month to the accounts payable subsidiary ledger. When posted a (✓) is placed in the PR column of the purchase journal for each transaction.

Purchase Journal

PR	Accounts Payable Cr.	Purchases Dr.	Sundry Dr.
✓ ✓ ✓	. . . .	. . . . . .	. . .
	. . . ( )	. . . ( )	. . . (X)

POSTED WHEN TRANSACTION IS ENTERED:
Post to general ledger account when transaction is entered.

The total of sundry is never posted.

END OF MONTH:
These totals are posted to the general ledger accounts at end of the month.
Examples: Accounts payable, purchases.

266

How to Post from Special Journals

Situation 6: Issuing a Debit Memo on Receiving a Credit Memo

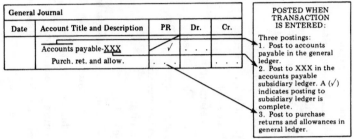

General Journal					
Date	Account Title and Description	PR	Dr.	Cr.
	Accounts payable-XXX	√	. . .	
	Purch. ret. and allow.	. . .		. . .

POSTED WHEN
TRANSACTION
IS ENTERED:

Three postings:
1. Post to accounts payable in the general ledger.
2. Post to XXX in the accounts payable subsidiary ledger. A (√) indicates posting to subsidiary ledger is complete.
3. Post to purchase returns and allowances in general ledger.

Situation 7: Outward Flow of Cash

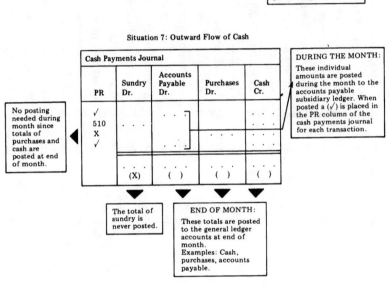

No posting needed during month since totals of purchases and cash are posted at end of month.

Cash Payments Journal					
	PR	Sundry Dr.	Accounts Payable Dr.	Purchases Dr.	Cash Cr.
	√	. . .	. . ⌐		. . .
	510				. . .
	X		. . .	. . .	. . .
	√		. . ⌐		. . .
		. . . (X)	( )	( )	( )

DURING THE MONTH:

These individual amounts are posted during the month to the accounts payable subsidiary ledger. When posted a (√) is placed in the PR column of the cash payments journal for each transaction.

The total of sundry is never posted.

END OF MONTH:

These totals are posted to the general ledger accounts at end of month.
Examples: Cash, purchases, accounts payable.

Student Summary Aid

Accounts	Increased by A:	Decreased by A:	Normal Balance	(Common Category)**
Accounts receivable	dr.	cr.	dr.	Current asset on balance sheet
Accounts payable	cr.	dr.	cr.	Current liability on balance sheet
Accumulated depreciation	cr.	dr.	cr.	Contra fixed asset on balance sheet
Allowance for doubtful account	cr.	dr.	cr.	Contra current asset on balance sheet
Bond payable	cr.	dr.	cr.	Current or long-term liability on balance sheet
Capital	cr.	dr.	cr.	Owner equity on the balance sheet
Capital stock	cr.	dr.	cr.	Stockholders' equity on balance sheet
Cash	dr.	cr.	dr.	Current asset on balance sheet
Common stock	cr.	dr.	cr.	Stockholders' equity on balance sheet
Common stock subscribed	cr.	dr.	cr.	Stockholders' equity on balance sheet
Common stock sub. receivable	dr.	cr.	dr.	Current asset on balance sheet
Depreciation expense	dr.	cr.	dr.	Expense on income statement
Discount on stock	dr.	cr.	dr.	Stockholders' equity on balance sheet
Dividends	dr.	cr.	dr.	A deduction from retained earnings
Dividend payable	cr.	dr.	cr.	Current liability on balance sheet
Drawings	dr.	cr.	dr.	A deduction from capital
Expired insurance	dr.	cr.	dr.	Expense on income statement
Freight-in	dr.	cr.	dr.	Part of costs of goods sold on income statement
Gain on disposal of equipment	cr.	dr.	cr.	Other income on income statement
Goodwill	dr.	cr.	dr.	Intangible asset on balance sheet
Interest expense	dr.	cr.	dr.	Other expenses on income statement
Interest income	cr.	dr.	cr.	Other income or revenue on income statement
Land	dr.	cr.	dr.	Fixed asset on balance sheet
Loss on disposal of equipment	dr.	cr.	dr.	Other expenses on income statement

Account			Classification
Merchandise inv. (get)	dr.	cr.	Current asset on balance sheet/Part of cost of goods sold on income statement
Mortgage note payable	cr.	dr.	Current or long-term liability on balance sheet
Notes payable	cr.	dr.	Current or long-term liability
Notes receivable	dr.	cr.	Current asset on balance sheet
Office supplies	dr.	cr.	Current asset on balance sheet
Organization cost	dr.	cr.	Intangible assets on balance sheet
Preferred stock	cr.	dr.	Stockholders' equity on balance sheet
Premium on stock	cr.	dr.	Stockholders' equity on balance sheet
Prepaid insurance	dr.	cr.	Current assets on balance sheet
Prepaid rent	dr.	cr.	Current asset on balance sheet
Purchases	dr.	cr.	Part of cost of goods sold on income statement
Purchase discount	cr.	dr.	Reduction of cost of goods sold on income statement
Purchase ret. & allowances	cr.	dr.	Reduction in cost of goods sold on income statement
Retained earnings	cr.	dr.	Stockholders' equity on balance sheet
Salary expense	dr.	cr.	Expense on income statement
Salaries payable?	cr.	dr.	Current liability on balance sheet
Sales	cr.	dr.	Revenue on income statement
Sales discount	dr.	cr.	Reduction of revenue on income statement
Sales ret. & allowance	dr.	cr.	Reduction of revenue on income statement
Sinking fund-cash	dr.	cr.	Other assets on balance sheet
Store supplies	dr.	cr.	Current asset on balance sheet
Treasury stock	dr.	cr.	Stockholders' equity on balance sheet
Unearned revenue	cr.	dr.	Current or long-term liabilities on balance sheet
Withdrawals	dr.	cr.	Reduction to capital

* Normal Balance = The usual balance that an account will have after all the increases and decreases (debits and credits) have been summarized. In text, see rules of debits and credits.

** Common Category.

1. Assets

   current (cash, acc. rec., notes rec., merchandise inv., prepaid expense, etc.)
   contra current (allowance for doubtful account)
   fixed assets (land, buildings, machinery, equipment, etc.)
   contra fixed asset (accumulated depreciation)
   intangible (patents, goodwill, organization costs, copyrights, etc.)

2. Liabilities

   current (notes payable, accounts payable, interest payable, etc.)
   long-term (notes payable, mortgage payable, bonds payable, etc.)

3. Owner equity (capital)
   ex: Russell State Capital   10,000

4. Stockholders' equity
   ex: common stock   12,000
        retained earnings   5,000
        Total stockholders' equity   17,000

5. Revenue (sales)

6. Expenses (heat)

7. Other (gains, losses, etc.)